LARRY RIVERS

"Not one day of my life have I wasted in searching for the truth." "I remember everything I know, even the most superficial things ... and what comes out is in my canvases." "I was energetic and egomaniacal and, what is more important, cocky and angry enough ..." "It's history that makes a person something."

LARRY RIVERS

Art and the Artist

FOREWORD BY DAVID C. LEVY

ESSAYS BY BARBARA ROSE

AND JACQUELYN DAYS SERWER

A BULFINCH PRESS BOOK

LITTLE, BROWN AND COMPANY

BOSTON   NEW YORK   LONDON

IN ASSOCIATION WITH

THE CORCORAN GALLERY OF ART

Black-and-white photographs not otherwise credited
are by unknown photographers and are from the
collection of Larry Rivers.

First Edition

ISBN 0-8212-2798-X (hardcover)
ISBN 0-8212-2824-2 (museum edition)
Library of Congress Control Number 2002102359

Bulfinch Press is an imprint and trademark of
Little, Brown and Company (Inc.)

PRINTED IN GERMANY

Front cover:
Plate 32, **The Greatest Homosexual,** 1964 (detail),
Hirshhorn Museum and Sculpture Garden, Smithsonian
Institution, Washington, D.C. Gift of Joseph H. Hirshhorn,
1966 (Photograph by Lee Stalsworth)

These pages:
Plate 22, **The Friendship of America and France
(Kennedy and De Gaulle),** 1961–62 (detail)

Following pages and back cover:
Rivers in his New York studio (David C. Levy)

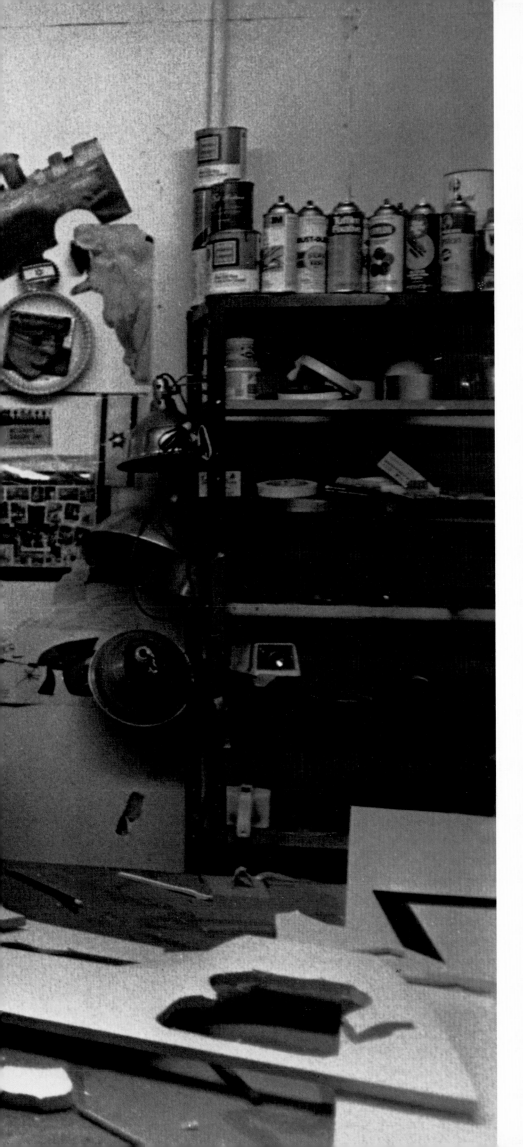

Contents

Acknowledgments

Many wonderful people have helped to make the Larry Rivers book and exhibition a reality. David Levy had conceived of such a show from the time he became president and director of the Corcoran Gallery of Art more than a decade ago. Barbara Rose, a friend and admirer of Rivers for over three decades, had always thought the Corcoran would be the perfect place to organize such a project. As a longtime fan of Rivers' work, I was happy to join them in such an exciting enterprise. Knowing also of Daniel Abadie, director of the Galerie Nationale du Jeu de Paume, in Paris, and his interest in Rivers' career, Rose suggested that the Corcoran and the Jeu de Paume collaborate in making this a truly memorable project reflective of Rivers' strong ties to French as well as American culture.

Certain individuals were indispensable in pulling together all the threads necessary to produce a major book in a relatively short time. Tracy Zungola, Rivers' archivist, spent untold hours gathering material, information, and photography, fulfilling an extraordinary number of requests over the course of a year and a half; the staff at New York's Marlborough Gallery, especially Bob Buck during his time there, the registrar, Kate Gilmartin, and Pierre Sebastian, responded to our needs with patience and professionalism. Jeffrey Loria and his staff, especially Julie Lavin, assisted us in many different ways with guidance, information, loans, and photography. Summer intern Mary Hendrickse assisted with general research as well as with the extensive chronology. My research assistant, Virginia Adams, was ingenious in ferreting out and verifying a dizzying array of information in record time. And my assistant, Amanda Zucker, was important to every aspect of the project, from handling the many organizational details to helping with the conceptualization of the exhibition and publication. I must also thank Jack Kirschbaum for helping to edit and shape the texts before they were delivered to the publisher.

The staff at the Hirshhorn Museum and Sculpture Garden of the Smithsonian Institution, which has an especially rich collection of works by Larry Rivers, offered information, expertise, and cooperation at many stages of the project. Judith Zilczer, curator of painting, arranged for us to view Rivers' works on more than one occasion and assisted with material on Rivers' *History of the Russian Revolution.* Phyllis Rosenzweig's 1982 catalog on the Rivers holdings constituted an invaluable resource, and registrar Anne-Louise Marquis provided the opportunity to examine works at length and to consult the Hirshhorn's collection of Rivers' archival materials.

At Bulfinch Press, encouraged by then-publisher Carol Leslie, our editor, Terry Hackford, believed in the project from the very beginning, and enlisted an outstanding team to produce this beautiful volume. Her assistant, Stephanie Lucianovic, production manager Sandra Klimt, and designer Susan Marsh have together created a book that reflects both Rivers' aesthetic and his remarkable career.

Lenders to the Exhibition

Happily, the current publisher, Jill Cohen, has continued Bulfinch's enthusiastic support for *Larry Rivers: Art and the Artist.*

Here at the Corcoran, the curatorial department performed brilliantly. Kimberly Davis, senior registrar, handled the extraordinarily complicated loan and shipping arrangements. Joan Oshinsky, traveling exhibition coordinator, worked to make the tour possible. Preparators Clyde Paton and David Jung were masterful in their solutions to our installation problems; and Elizabeth Parr, exhibitions director, working with designer Linda Rice, supervised every aspect of the exhibition design and installation.

I must thank our lenders, listed here, for their generosity in allowing us to feature major works from both public and private collections. I also wish to express our gratitude to the Friends of The Corcoran Gallery of Art, who have generously funded the Rivers exhibition at the Corcoran.

Last, I want to express my deep appreciation to Larry Rivers. For more than half a century he has devoted himself to producing art that has both enhanced our lives and helped to make sense of our world.

Jacquelyn Days Serwer

Chief Curator
The Corcoran Gallery of Art

Giovanni Agnelli, La Stampa, Turin, Italy
Anderson Gallery, Buffalo, New York
Andrea Bollt, New York
Centre Georges Pompidou, Paris
The Cheekwood Museum of Art, Nashville, Tennessee
Colby College Museum of Art, Waterville, Maine
The Corcoran Gallery of Art, Washington, D.C.
Fort Wayne Museum of Art, Fort Wayne, Indiana
Frederick R. Weissman Art Foundation, Los Angeles
The Harry N. Abrams Family Collection, New York
Hirshhorn Museum and Sculpture Garden,
    Smithsonian Institution, Washington, D.C.
Jan Turner Gallery, Los Angeles, California
David C. Levy, Washington, D.C.
Marlborough Gallery, New York
Risa Meyers, New York
The Minneapolis Institute of Arts, Minneapolis
Museo de Arte Contemporáneo, Caracas, Venezuela
The Museum of Modern Art, New York
The National Gallery of Art, Washington, D.C.
The Nelson-Atkins Museum of Art, Kansas City, Missouri
Neuberger Museum, Purchase, New York
The Parrish Art Museum, Southampton, New York
Private Collection, New Jersey
Private Collection, New York
Larry Rivers, New York
Richard Shebairo, New York
Mark and Livia Straus, Chappaqua, New York
Tate Modern Museum, Bankside, London
Tibor de Nagy Gallery, New York
Mr. and Mrs. Richard Titelman, Atlanta, Georgia
United States Holocaust Memorial Museum, Washington, D.C.
Universal Limited Art Editions, Bay Shore, New York
The Whitney Museum of American Art, New York
Williams College Museum of Art, Williamstown, Massachusetts

Foreword: My Friendship with Larry Rivers

DAVID C. LEVY

PRESIDENT AND DIRECTOR

THE CORCORAN GALLERY OF ART

On a chilly morning

in the early spring of 1974, I climbed the six flights to Larry Rivers' block-long studio and loft on Manhattan's Lower East Side. Thus began one of the closest friendships of my life. My purpose was to recruit Rivers to teach in a new fine arts major at Parsons School of Design. I had become the head of Parsons a year earlier, and my first thought had been to reestablish programs in painting and sculpture that had been abandoned in the beginning decades of the century, after the departure of the school's founder, William Merritt Chase. I wanted this new program to have a faculty that resonated with the unique resources of New York and the energy of its art community.

Rivers in his studio,
Southampton, 2000
(David C. Levy)

Larry Rivers seemed exactly the right person with whom to start. A founding father of pop, he seemed more inventive and in the long view more influential than others, like Andy Warhol or Roy Lichtenstein, who, although iconic figures in the movement, were more narrowly focused and had not yet outgrown either the pop label or its signature style. In addition, Rivers' technical abilities, particularly his drawing, were astonishing. They represented a much-needed breath of fresh air in the aftermath of abstract expressionism, which by the mid-1960s had produced a generation of artist-teachers with skills so limited that they were forced as a matter of self-protection to proclaim technique, particularly drawing, dead. This was doing damage to art schools, their curricula, and their students. Finally, I saw in Rivers' work a creative bridge between the greatest traditions of painting and a contemporary no-holds-barred irreverence that spoke to the times and to the real achievements of American art in the 1950s and 1960s.

As I climbed those stairs, though, I had little reason to believe that Rivers (whom I had never met) would accept my request to join the Parsons faculty. In those early days we didn't pay much and, perhaps even more problematic, we had a brand-new program with no upper-level students. So I was about to ask one of the most celebrated artists of our time to teach Painting 101 to sophomores for a good deal less money than he could make at home in his studio between breakfast and midmorning coffee.

Our meeting that day is burned into my memory. We sat at a cluttered, forbiddingly angular metal table, which Larry proudly told me he had designed himself (remember, Parsons School of *Design*), and we talked about jazz. Like Larry, I too had begun my career as a jazz musician, and this was later to become an important bond between us.

But the jazz talk on this particular morning didn't go so well. Larry praised the legendary saxophonist John Coltrane and I opined that, while I recognized it to be heresy, I found his playing distinctly unmusical. Larry replied that under those circumstances he could think of nothing further to say to me.

So I was more than a little surprised when he agreed to teach. Later he wrote in his autobiography that he did it for the health insurance, which seems improbable until you recognize his acute degree of hypochondria, a preoccupation only partially based on the fact that he actually does have a number of long-term medical problems. As they say, even paranoids have real enemies.

Our relationship deepened as Larry began to teach the following fall. He was a veteran of many short visiting artist stints, but the responsibility for a regular class of undergraduates was new for him, and working with relatively young and inexperienced kids was certainly uncharted territory.

A frequent visitor to his classroom, I discovered qualities in this man that drew me to him in unexpected ways. He was, for example, amazingly patient with his students. His class was their first exposure to real painting, and they needed a lot of basic work. So he spent a couple of weeks teaching them how to stretch canvas. Attracted one morning by the unusual racket, I was astounded to find him on his hands and knees happily surrounded by nineteen-year-olds hammering tacks into stretchers.

I understood this impulse better a few months later when we were together on a flight to Detroit. A child was running noisily back and forth creating a ruckus that heralded the beginning of a two-and-a-half-hour flight from hell. This vision was dispelled, however, when Larry joined the boy on the floor of the aisle, gleefully making funny faces and keeping him amused, to the great pleasure of them both.

The East Thirteenth Street Band (from left): Howard Brofsky, David Levy, Paul Brown, Phoebe Legere, Earl Williams, Larry Rivers, Charles Toor, Howard Kanovitz

Discovering Larry's love of children was only one of many small revelations that helped me understand the warmth, loyalty, and occasional sentimentality that are part of the more private side of his complicated, protean, and publicly irreverent personality.

A defining moment that perhaps more than any other single event was to shape our relationship over time was, again, about music. A couple of years after Larry joined the faculty, somebody suggested that we put together a band for Parsons' popular potluck Christmas party. So I gathered up a few of the musician folks with whom I had been on the road years earlier. Larry showed up with an old C-melody saxophone, and we brought the house down. Truth be told, the music was terrible. But the experience was enough to encourage us to start playing again. Larry's C-melody, however, was a serious impediment. The instrument has been obsolete since the 1930s, and for good reason. So a month or so later I took the opportunity to repay a generous favor and bought him a present – a B-flat tenor sax.

The new horn permitted Larry to play seriously with a group for the first time in years, and soon we started to meet regularly in his Thirteenth Street loft, joined by friends who like us had professional music in their backgrounds. Painter Howard Kanovitz, who had played trombone with Gene Krupa, was a regular, as was James Joyce scholar

and Romare Bearden biographer Myron Schwartzman, an accomplished jazz pianist with whom I had worked in and out of New York years earlier.

We started out just for the fun of it but quickly began writing original material, which transformed jam sessions into rehearsals. Soon we played for a party or two and suddenly found ourselves with a tightly rehearsed seven-piece band that was much in demand in New York and, ultimately, all over the country. We even made occasional commercial recordings and toured as far as the Caribbean. During the 1980s the East Thirteenth Street Band was definitely a hit, and Larry and I were probably working as much as any full-time jazz musicians in New York. The difference was that those guys slept all day. We had other things to do. It was a heady and exhilarating time.

The point here is not that the band made particularly good music but that it became an intense and fulfilling focus of our personal lives. It was, in effect, our family. This was important, because at the time our real family lives were in flux. Our kids were growing up and leaving home, marriages were uncertain or failing, and we needed an emotional anchor. As with all families, though, things were not always smooth, and I recall a phone call from Larry following a particularly acrimonious band meltdown in which he described it as the most important thing in our lives, vowing that it had to be preserved at all costs.

Looking back, I find this period one of great productivity for both Larry and me. He painted with a steady intensity that produced an astonishing amount of important work, including such series of works as *The Coloring Book of Japan, History of Matzoh, Golden Oldies, The Continuing Interest in Abstract Art,* and *Public and Private.* I was helping to build Parsons from a small school of 500 students to a virtual arts university with an enrollment of 12,000 and campuses in New York, California, Paris, Japan, and the Dominican Republic. Larry and I spoke daily on the phone, sometimes about art, politics, sex, and automobiles, but always about music and women.

Larry has always insisted that an artist's work should stand by itself. If knowing the history or psychology of the artist is a requirement for understanding, he says, then the art has failed. Nevertheless, it is revealing to explore the restless complexity and unusual intellectual depth of this artist, because it helps explain the ways in which his long career has unfolded and puts both his work and his life in a useful social and professional perspective.

Several characteristics appear to have determined the course of Larry Rivers' career. First, he is a visual natural. This is the source of his technical mastery and elegant draftsmanship, which certainly were not products of his study with abstract expressionist guru Hans Hofmann. Second, he is an intellectual. Literature, politics, and words are as important to him as paint and canvas. An obsessive reader, he makes subtle, educated connections between ideas and information. Third, he is constitutionally restless, never satisfied with one idea or theme in his work. The outcome in this instance has not always been positive. Although the overall graph of Rivers' development reveals both continuity and evolution, it is regularly punctuated by darts and deviations from the centerline, exploring this new technique, that imagery, or some ism or other that may momentarily have captured his imagination.

One outcome of such restless experimentation has been a number of failures. He does not like to concede them publicly, but he is both mature and honest enough to admit them to himself. As a result he has never followed dead-end enthusiasms or

blind alleys for long, nor has he lacked the inner guidance to bring himself back on track. Thus his work follows a steady, richly rewarding evolutionary progression.

I had an insight into Larry's self-awareness when the huge Picasso retrospective opened at the Museum of Modern Art in 1980. We both attended a packed black-tie opening party, and at some point in the evening I lost track of him. The next morning he called, and when I asked what had become of him the night before, he said he had gone home halfway through the show. Picasso did "so many different things," Larry said, "and all of them *worked!* I got so depressed I just had to leave."

To understand the New York art world in which Larry Rivers came of age during the 1950s, it helps to remember that the emergence of abstract expressionism in the late 1940s began a decade and a half of unyielding orthodoxy in American art. Led by such high priests as Clement Greenberg and Harold Rosenberg, the movement permitted virtually no other approach among the cognoscenti. In this context, Rivers' early success was extraordinary, not simply because his star rose so rapidly but because the path he chose was, for those times, dangerous and challenging. Unlike that of his pop colleagues later on, his work was not conventionally unconventional. In fact, his originality went far deeper, because in works like the early portraits of Berdie and the great painting of Frank O'Hara he was bending long-standing traditions and dazzling technique to subtly new expressive ends – a more difficult creative task, less easily understood within the context of reigning critical fashion than the in-your-face iconoclasm of pop.

Pop, however, introduced an important new variable that hastened the end of abstract expressionism's stranglehold and helped to rekindle an

Larry Rivers, acquaintance Jackie Curtis, and David C. Levy, president and director of the Corcoran Gallery of Art, 1981

interest in figurative, or at least representational, painting. Larry Rivers played a central role in this critical reawakening. One might say that for the ten to fifteen years of abstract expressionist ascendancy, artists looked inward, trying to identify and depict psychological and emotional truths not found in normal visual experience. Whatever their revelations may have been, they were certainly not part of the visual world that surrounds ordinary mortals. By the early 1960s this had created what might be called a Rip Van Winkle effect. In other words, as abstract expressionism began to lose its momentum, a new generation of artists awoke, opening fresh eyes in a world that had been transformed during their aesthetic slumber by an explosion of advertising imagery, the emergence of television, and the graphic design of popular culture. It is not a great leap to see how logical, appealing, or even *conventional* it would be to make these ubiquitous commercial images the subjects of a new art, picking up and extending ideas that had first been explored before World War II by such artists as Stuart Davis and Gerald Murphy.

With this in mind, Warhol's Brillo boxes, Lichtenstein's comics, or Jasper Johns' bronze-cast beer cans are simple distillations. Rivers, on the other hand, along with Robert Rauschenberg, had a more complex and subtle vision of pop. In their hands it

became a stylistic gestalt that encompassed a far broader range of subject, media, and technique.

Larry's decision not to run completely with the pop pack is all the more interesting because he was something of a What Makes Sammy Run kid from the Bronx. Conventional and financial success were, and remain, very important to him. In this regard he is reminiscent of Edouard Manet, who a hundred years earlier aspired to become a respected academic artist and successfully began his career along that path. But Manet, like Rivers, was driven by inner convictions to produce work that alienated the establishment he wished so much to please. Of course in Rivers' case he *did* succeed, but in retrospect it seems almost an accident, and there is little question that had he been willing to play the art-world game a little harder, his success would have been even greater.

To the degree, however, that an artist can be judged by his influence on others and on history, Larry Rivers takes a place of seminal importance in American art during the second half of the twentieth century. The mainstream of pop, though perhaps the most promising movement of the last forty years, for the most part created priests, not prophets. By contrast, Rivers' impact has already reverberated powerfully through several generations and has been of great importance to artistic development both in America and in Europe.

As the following pages document, Larry Rivers' work spans fifty years of restless exploration, consummate skill, and deep insight. Artist, musician, intellectual, hypochondriac, and friend, he is one of the great creative talents of our time and has made a lasting and profound contribution to our cultural heritage.

Larry Rivers: Painter of Modern Life

BARBARA ROSE

Sometimes he may be a poet; more often he comes close to the novelist. . . .

He is the painter of the fleeting moment and of all that it suggests of the eternal.

— CHARLES BAUDELAIRE, "THE PAINTER OF MODERN LIFE"[1]

Yitzroch Loiza Grossberg was born

in the Bronx on August 17, 1923, to Samuel (Shiah) and Shirley (Sonya)

Grossberg, Jewish immigrants from the Ukraine. Sam was a plumber who

worked up to being an entrepreneur as the owner of a small trucking

firm. He gave his oldest child music lessons so the boy could accompany

him when he played the violin at family functions. At the age of seven,

like so many of the children of the culturally sophisticated Eastern

European Jews who immigrated to the United States, Yitzroch began

piano lessons. Piano and violin, however, were the instruments of

classical and European music. Young Yitzroch (who was already calling

himself Irving as a child) was determined to be an all-American boy.

Young Rivers playing
the saxophone

American music was not the soulful lament of the ghetto but the intense sexually charged rhythmic beat of jazz. The brilliant and precocious boy soon realized that the classical music of America had roots not in Europe but in Africa. In his passion for American culture and his determination to be part of it, before long Yitzroch gave up the piano for the saxophone. A year before his bar mitzvah, he was already playing jazz saxophone in borscht circuit resorts in the Catskills. Seven years later he did two dramatic things: he changed his name to Larry Rivers, and he enlisted in the U.S. Army Air Corps to fight Hitler. The nervous, multitalented young man's life would continue to be dramatic and surprising, in its own way a kind of heroic resistance, but he would never become known for his contributions either to music or warfare. His lasting contribution would be to art history as the originator of the imagery of pop art and as a painter who held fast to Jean-Dominique Ingres's idea that drawing is the probity of art.

An early experience that marked Rivers as a mature artist was watching James Michael Newell paint the WPA mural cycle documenting the history of American culture that still decorates the library of Evander Childs, the Bronx high school Rivers attended. These were the first history paintings that Rivers saw. As he himself observed, they made an indelible impression.[2] Twenty years later Rivers painted *Washington Crossing the Delaware* (Pl. 3), a sketchy, expressionist parody of Emanuel Leutze's 1851 academic depiction of the historic moment in the American Revolution that is one of the most popular pictures in the Metropolitan Museum.

A huge machine painting in the detailed realism of the Davidian Beaux Arts style in its decadent academic phase, *Washington Crossing the Delaware* was the ideal subject to express the love-hate relationship with tradition that marks Rivers' life as well as his style as an artist. A second version, painted in 1960 after the original was damaged in the Museum of Modern Art fire of 1958, is a painterly pastiche of images stolen from Leonardo da Vinci and a children's book that intermingles high and low culture in a typical Rivers minestrone of styles and periods.

The mixed message of admiration and travesty typical of Rivers' reworking of the old masters can be characterized as a version of the camp sensibility, which affectionately impersonates the original inspiration rather than attacking in bitter antagonistic satire. The pop artists inspired by Rivers, on the other hand, were ironic and deadpan in their paraphrases of art historical precedents, which the generation after them turned into cynical appropriation of reproduced images. Rivers' approach is far more innocent and playful. His criticism is not of consumerism but of orthodoxy and convention, whether in art or in life.

Jazz Musician, 1958
Oil on canvas
70 x 58 in.
Private Collection, New York

Formed by the Marxist and social realist concerns of the 1930s, Rivers emerged as a painter of popular democratic subject matter in the early 1950s. Rivers' unique ability to paint multifigure compositions set him apart from the New York School, as did his interest in the sources of modernism. Transforming the slick varnished surfaces of Leutze's original salon painting into sketchy patches, he repeats Courbet's and Manet's criticism of academic painting, but this time in the new idiom of the American vernacular. His reinterpretation is fraught with ambiguity, either intentionally or unintentionally, with regard to its relationship not only to French salon painting but also to the loose painterly style of Courbet and Manet that ushered in the modernism that opposed it. It is as if in the old battle of ancients versus moderns, Rivers wanted to fight on both sides. The mockery of the epic ideals of academic history painting is ambiguously combined with an admiration for its heroic ambition. But ambiguity – sexual, cultural, and artistic – was characteristic of Rivers. For it was inevitable that the child of immigrants, who was crazy about American popular culture, from the movies to jazz and rock and roll, should be confused

as he struggled to construct an identity out of fantasies of the glamour of Parisian *vie bohème.*

As a patriotic American, Rivers enlisted, but in 1943 he was honorably discharged, diagnosed with multiple sclerosis. The diagnosis was mistaken, but to this day he still has a slight tremor in his left hand. Unlike the other second-generation New York School painters who were in the army at the end of the war, he did not qualify for the generous GI Bill, which enabled an entire generation of Americans to study abroad. However, his disability pension permitted him to study music theory and composition at the Juilliard School of Music. As the war came to a close he toured with various jazz bands. At Juilliard he met the legendary trumpet player Miles Davis, who introduced him to other jazz musicians in the underground, mainly from the black world of cool jazz.

The year World War II ended, Rivers married Augusta Burger, the mother of an infant son, Joseph, whom Rivers adopted. Together the young couple had another son, Steven. Augusta and Larry, who was earning a wretched living as a musician, would separate in 1946. While touring the resort circuit with his band in the summer of 1945, he met a young painter named Jane Freilicher in Old Orchard Beach, Maine. Her husband, Jack, played piano in the band. Jane encouraged Larry to pursue his artistic talent. Under her tutelage he began to paint and sketch in a primitive, almost cartoonlike style. Back in New York that fall, Freilicher introduced the young man to the painter Nell Blaine. The next year, having separated from his wife, Rivers moved to a studio on East Twenty-first Street, the area where Blaine and Freilicher also had studios.

A year older than Rivers, Blaine already had a significant reputation in New York. A student of Hans Hofmann, Blaine was caught, as was Hofmann

Jane Freilicher
*Still Life with
Calendulas,* 1955
Oil on canvas
65½ x 49½ in.
Collection Elizabeth
Hazan
Courtesy Tibor de Nagy
Gallery, New York

Nell Blaine,
Red and Black, 1945
Oil on canvas
23 x 20 in.
Collection The Judith
Rothschild Foundation
Courtesy Tibor de Nagy
Gallery, New York

himself, between abstraction and figuration, although her work in the early 1940s was a form of painterly abstraction. She was an abstract painter when Peggy Guggenheim included her in her "Women" show at *Art of This Century* in 1943. Blaine was also a member of the Jane Street Gallery, a co-op where artists indebted to Léger, Mondrian, and Helion's biomorphism showed. Blaine, however, was a painterly painter whose heroes were de Kooning and Bonnard. A jazz aficionado, she painted an homage to saxophone player Lester Young that anticipates Rivers' series of portraits of jazz musicians.

In 1947 Blaine persuaded Rivers and Freilicher to enroll in Hofmann's art school on Eighth Street, which was in many respects the epicenter of the New York art world. Among his students were Robert De Niro, father of the actor, and many budding New York School talents like Lee Krasner. Hofmann's teaching emphasized drawing as the fundamental element in art. His theories were based on a synthesis of ideas taken from Matisse, Kandinsky, and Mondrian. A refugee from Hitler's Germany, Hofmann insisted that his students work, like Cézanne, *devant le motif.* The objective, however, was not to turn them into figurative artists but to teach the dynamism of spatial relations through the study of still life, the human figure, and landscape.

Hofmann's Provincetown summer school stressed landscape. In New York students worked from still life setups as well as from live models. "My problem back then in 1947," Rivers remembers, "was that when I started drawing in the presence of a nude female model, all that found its way onto my pages were three peculiar rectangles. At the end of a year I became frantic to draw the figure. . . . If I didn't do this, I'd never be able to convince myself of my genius. . . . It was important

to me to solidify my position, to be able to say, yes, don't worry, you are really an artist."[3] While Hofmann's fellow countryman Josef Albers taught mechanistic grid-based Bauhaus design and color theory at Black Mountain College in Asheville, North Carolina, to artists like Robert Rauschenberg and Kenneth Noland, Hofmann developed a color theory that had roots not in the neo-impressionist theory of optical mixture, but in the earlier tradition established by Roger de Piles. In his manual on color theory, a bible for artists from Rubens through Delacroix, de Piles emphasized the opposition of warm and cool colors to create spatial tension. Essentially bringing de Piles's color theory up to date, Hofmann, who became an abstract artist only in the last decade of his long life, developed the idea of "push-pull" to create space through color. This opposition was based on the properties of warm colors to advance and cool hues to recede. Despite his emphasis on color, Hofmann stressed that drawing was the fundamental element in painting, a lesson that Rivers never forgot.

It was clear to the other students as well as to Hofmann that Rivers had exceptional talent. What Rivers actually learned from Hofmann, however, is questionable. Aside from his theories of art, like

push and pull, Rivers confided to Frank O'Hara, "Hans Hofmann made art glamorous by including in the same sentence with the names Michelangelo, Rubens, Courbet, and Matisse, the name Rivers and his own, of course. It wasn't that you were a Michelangelo or a Matisse, but that you faced somewhat similar problems. What he really did by talking this way was to inspire you to work."[4] Rivers stayed with Hofmann for two years.

During his student years Rivers painted small cubist-derived oils. Clearly he was in search of a role model to inspire him in the development of a personal style. Hofmann's students did not see his own painting, so clearly he could not be that inspiration. In 1948 the Museum of Modern Art held a Bonnard retrospective. For Rivers, who called the exhibition a "milestone" in his life, it was a turning point that proved that modernism was not incompatible with figuration. Hardly a traditional realist, Bonnard represented a painterly version of figuration which convinced Rivers that representational art need not be academic. This was important, because at that moment the New York School was going resolutely toward abstraction.

Inspired by Bonnard, but still very much in the milieu of the Hofmann school, Rivers began to paint high-keyed impressionistic still lifes and studio interiors. He showed these in the spring of 1949 in his first one-person exhibition, which Blaine arranged for him at the Jane Street Gallery. Clement Greenberg, who had attended Hofmann's lectures in the 1930s, wrote an enthusiastic review in *The Nation.* In the spring of 1950 Greenberg and Meyer Schapiro chose to include him in the prestigious New Talent exhibition they jointly curated for the Kootz Gallery.

Around this time, Rivers decided that he had to prepare for a more secure profession to be able to

Burial Study II
Charcoal on paper
12 ½ × 11 in.
The Jewish Museum, New York
Gift of Mrs. Samuel H. Gifford in
Memory of Alfred W. Kleinbaum,
by exchange

support his two sons, who lived with him rather than their mother. Rivers registered in the art education program at New York University so that he could, if necessary, become a teacher. He received a B.A. three years later. At NYU he studied with William Baziotes, and his fellow students included Robert Goodnough and Alfred Leslie. The campus at Washington Square was in the middle of Greenwich Village, not far from the infamous artists' hangout the Cedar Bar.

During this time Rivers met Willem de Kooning and other New York artists and poets who became lifelong friends. Through them he was introduced to the lively scene at East Hampton, where, beginning with Jackson Pollock, who moved to the Long Island town in 1946, artists took refuge from the city. In 1950 Rivers went to Europe to

study the old masters firsthand, visiting Italy and spending eight crucial months in Paris. He returned a changed man. His new heroes were Courbet and Manet. In honor of his grandmother's funeral, he painted *The Burial* (page 71), a gloomy picture inspired by the dark palette and visible impasto of Courbet's *A Burial at Ornans.* Rivers also painted an interpretation of Manet's *Luncheon on the Grass* as a kind of depressed picnic.

The Burial was Rivers' most ambitious painting to date. It was exhibited in his first show at the Tibor de Nagy Gallery in 1951. The gallery director, John Bernard Myers, was a cultured intellectual who would also publish the New York poets. He quickly became devoted to Rivers' cause as an artist, and he also fell madly in love with the ebullient, good-looking young man. When Rivers left the gallery in 1963 to join the more prestigious and affluent Marlborough Gallery (then called Marlborough-Gerson), on Fifty-seventh Street, Myers was outraged by Rivers' betrayal and arrived at his opening with a summons. The move broke up their friendship, but Myers consistently championed Rivers, and Rivers acknowledged the important role that Myers played in his career.

Often Myers was Rivers' model. Once he posed for all twelve disciples in a version of *The Agony in the Garden.* Rivers also made sketches, portraits, and a sculpture bust of Myers, which was cast in bronze. As the office boy at *View,* the magazine the surrealists published in New York in the 1940s, Myers had become an authority on free association, which he encouraged in Rivers. For Myers, the younger man was a quintessential beatnik. "If ever there was a Beat, it was Rivers. . . . The distance, the skepticism, the refusal to be in one place, the denial of all middle-class values, even the [surrealistic] process of suspending consciousness to dredge up one's own resources."[5] Later on, Myers observed that Rivers cultivated going against the grain in the sense of Des Esseintes, hero of Huysmàns' novel *À rebours.* Indeed perverse subversion, not only of art history but of himself as well, is central to Rivers' complex, contradictory personality.

ENTER THE WUNDERKIND

A lot of people I know are at the edge of complete disintegration and want to give life up or trade it in at any moment; I'm at the edge.
– LARRY RIVERS, 1951[6]

In his book on the recurrence of style and form throughout the history of art, *The Shape of Time,* George Kubler describes the appearance of an artist whose talents and personality coincided with the zeitgeist of the moment as making a "propitious entrance" onto the stage of art history. In many respects Larry Rivers made such an entrance. The critics found much to praise in Rivers' first show at the Tibor de Nagy Gallery. According to the exigent Manny Farber, "Rivers was a twenty-eight-year-old romantic . . . bleeding with compassion and bursting with bravura." The works on view reflected "the several depots of his jolting journey – the Bronx, Hans Hofmann assembly line, the new Bohemia." He saw Rivers as "a rare natural dauber – a painter's painter on the order of Bonnard and Rouault, if you can imagine such a slapstick marriage."[7]

Farber describes Rivers' "Faulkner-like view of local [New York] misery – turmoil, exasperation, nostalgia; lesbians, rabbis, Fire Island cottages, all tied together by a tireless, gushing, rhetorical cross-hatching of strokes." Farber saw Rivers' impetuous all-over pattern of brush texture as "Bonnard's

spots blown up into broccoli." He had, of course, a few reservations, accusing Rivers of slamming together "endless combinations of pure pigment working always for total ripeness with an unpleasant mustardy tone and sweat." Despite these caveats, Farber, a gifted painter himself, was certain that "the paintings at the Tibor de Nagy indicate that he is only a year or so away from a top position in avant-garde art if he doesn't waste away in jitters and torment."[8]

The perpetually jittery and tormented Rivers nevertheless wasted no time in fulfilling Farber's prophecy. He began to do sculpture as well as to paint and draw. By the time he joined Myers' gallery in 1951, Rivers had found a loft at 122 Second Avenue, on Manhattan's Lower East Side, where he began a series of figure sculptures, many life-size or larger, modeled in a mixture of plaster, cement, and sand, and then carved. The figures, according to Fairfield Porter, suggested the lava-encrusted, preserved bodies from Herculaneum and Pompeii.[9] The plaster sculptures were naive, but by the time Rivers worked up to casting in bronze, he was able to manipulate surfaces and to capture the sitters' likenesses.

By 1952 Rivers' style had loosened up considerably in response to de Kooning's influence. De Kooning had become a good friend and Rivers, like much of the second generation of the New York School, his avid admirer. However, the part of de Kooning's style that appealed to Rivers was not the bodily gesture of "action painting" but his drawing and his depiction of the human body as a series of summary slashes and strokes. A de Kooning painting like *Pink Angels,* for example, with its figurative source barely hidden and its funky pink and mustard palette, was an obvious inspiration for Rivers during this period.

Rivers with one of his sculptures

When Rivers' new paintings were shown at the Tibor de Nagy Gallery in the winter of 1952 they drew general praise. Stuart Preston of the *New York Times* described Rivers' style as "realism expressed in the abstract manner of today . . . uniting sinuous brush strokes with moody, low-key color."[10] Goodnough, who also showed at the gallery, stressed the subjective qualities of the paintings: "The pictures are made up of strongly felt areas of paint that move well in relation to the entire surface of the canvas. It is here that their quality lies, for while most of the paintings are of massive figures, the figure seems to be there only to support the artist's emotional expression. Paint areas are organized into masses that move intensely and passionately into one another."[11]

As a talented figure painter of his generation, Rivers won universal high praise. When he began to show signs, however, not only of nonconformism but of a megalomaniacal ambition that dared to challenge the old masters, he exhibited intolerable hubris, which was bound to elicit hostility. Thus when Myers exhibited *Washington Crossing the Delaware* in December 1953, the critical reviews

were mixed but basically favorable. The response of Rivers' peers, on the other hand, was not.

According to Rivers, the reaction to his interpretation of the hack salon cliché was about the same reaction as when the Dadaists introduced a toilet seat as a piece of sculpture in a Dada show in Zurich. Except that the public wasn't upset – the painters were. "One painter, Gandy Brodie, who was quite forceful, called me a phony. In the bar where I can usually be found, a lot of painters laughed."[12] Rivers was crushed by the rejection of his peers at the Cedar Bar, who were mainly abstract artists. He felt that he should have been accepted since, in the end, he identified much more with them than with the artists who were painting realistically.

A younger generation, however, was fascinated by Rivers' irreverent treatment of popular subject. For example, Roy Lichtenstein was inspired to paint his own Klee-like interpretation of the scene, which could be considered his first pop painting. Certainly the mock-heroic style that Rivers was practicing had no place in the philosophically pretentious high culture tone of the New York School. It was instead a bold move against abstraction at the height of its triumph.

Rivers' style exposed the underlying ambivalence of the New York School toward abstract art. That ambivalence can be seen in the conversion of Rivers' friend Alfred Leslie, then gaining fame as a second-generation action painter, to realism in the mid-1960s. A decade earlier Rivers' George Washington had inspired Leslie to take a stab at history painting in a portrait of Henry Ford with his Model T. Harry Jackson, a Pollock imitator at the time married to Grace Hartigan, gave up dripping to devote himself to the study of Courbet. His first realist painting, apparently also inspired by the same Rivers work, was *Custer's Last Stand.*

Jackson went on to become a popular and fashionable painter of western themes. Leslie, on the other hand, stunned by the Caravaggio retrospective of 1966, had a more serious conversion to representational art. When Frank O'Hara died that year in an accident – a jeep hit him while he was strolling on the beach at Fire Island – Leslie began a series of moving interpretations of Caravaggio's *Deposition* as the tragic *Death of Frank O'Hara.*

In his use of preexisting imagery and rejection of abstract art as too pure and remote, Rivers shares with Jasper Johns and Rauschenberg the role of effecting the transition from the hermeticism of abstract expressionism to a more directly accessible type of representational art. Like them, he combines the refined painterly brushwork of the New York School with the subject matter of common objects. His style, like theirs, exhibits a symbiosis with printmaking techniques and processes that defines a new attitude toward representation in post-abstract painting. According to Rivers, what they had in common was an admiration of the giants of the New York School and an unwillingness to repeat them.[13]

PAINTER AMONG POETS

I thought of a picture as a surface the eye travels over in order to find delicacies to munch on; sated, it moves on to the next part in whatever order it wishes. A smorgasbord of the recognizable, and if being the chef is no particular thrill, it was as much as I could cook up. — LARRY RIVERS, 1961[14]

If Guillaume Apollinaire won fame as the poet among painters, then Rivers surely deserves the epithet painter among poets. Throughout his life he has been closer to poets than to painters. Indeed, he originally aspired to be a poet. The New York poetry world of the 1950s was as split as the art world was between the bohemian downtown action painters and the uptown intellectual chromatic abstractionists. The so-called New York poets, including John Ashbery, Kenneth Koch, and Frank O'Hara, were Harvard graduates who came down from Cambridge to New York in the late 1940s; the Beat poets, on the other hand, who migrated to New York from San Francisco in the early 1950s, included Jack Kerouac, Allen Ginsberg, and Gregory Corso. Rivers was the only person who bridged the gap between them, equally attracted to the elegance of the New York poets as to the Whitmanesque excesses of the Beats. In 1959 Rivers had his beatitude certified by appearing in the underground classic film *Pull My Daisy,* made by Robert Frank and Alfred Leslie, with a cast that included the Beat poets.

Frank O'Hara met Rivers in 1950 at a cocktail party. He recalled Rivers waving at the crowd, proclaiming, "After all it's life we're interested in, not art." A few weeks later, when O'Hara visited Rivers' studio for the first time, the voluble painter said, as O'Hara recalled, "with no air of contradiction or remembrance, 'After all, it's art we're interested in, not life.' His main interest was obviously in the immediate situation."[15] O'Hara made Rivers more aware of poetry and provided him with a good audience. This gave Rivers the confidence to take himself more seriously.

The New York School poets worshiped Apollinaire and his embrace of the popular subject matter of modern Paris. They imitated his style in a way that could be characterized as high camp. The camp sensibility, a mixed message of admiration and parody, also typifies Rivers' reworking of the old masters. Camp first elevated cliché to the level of the sublime. Impersonation and travesty are central elements of camp, which mixes an arch playfulness with nostalgic, even romantic sentiment.

Rivers, always ready to outrage, has more in common with the underground camp sensibility than he does with the stinging irony of pop art. Picasso's biographer John Richardson first identified this element in Rivers' work.[16] The camp sensibility as defined by Susan Sontag is certainly at work in Rivers' appropriation and often humorous interpretation of the imagery of the masters of painterly painting in a spirit that is neither ironic nor mocking.[17] Rivers' camp interpretation of the familiar historic event in the career of America's founding father undoubtedly questions the notion of the heroic and epic pretensions of the New York School.

The role of reproduction was crucial to the purveyors of popular imagery who succeeded Rivers. He instead studied the originals, not their reproductions. He haunted museums and traveled widely in Europe. His surfaces are not the slick uninflected mechanical surfaces of graphics or advertising, but the clearly hand-painted and sensually textured surfaces we associate with old master painting itself, experienced directly rather than through a media filter.

That Rivers chose to consort with poets and writers was looked on with some suspicion by the art-for-art purists seeing the narrative element in his art as the adulteration of formal concerns. Early on they began to consider him a betrayer of the lofty ideals of the New York School. The literary content of Rivers' work became increasingly prominent the more he was criticized for it. More material from his everyday life found its way into his paintings as a conscious rejection of the tenets of formalism, which held that any literary content was inimical to

high modernism. He was the art rebel with a cause, which was the thoroughly unfashionable one of drawing, hand painting, and the observation of daily life that Robert Henri had counseled was the essence of art. In the atmosphere of the New York School, that counted as treason.

If the painters looked at him suspiciously, he would take succor in the company of poets. A neighbor of Jane Freilicher, Kenneth Koch had just graduated from Harvard when he met Rivers in 1948. He was immediately impressed by Rivers' Bonnard-style interiors. The only one extant, *Still Life with Knoll Table,* shows a young artist apprenticing himself to the School of Paris master. Ashbery, who like Baudelaire before him earned a living as an art critic, became a friend and supporter of Rivers' exceptional talent and obvious virtuosity. O'Hara was named a curator at the Museum of Modern Art, even though he had studied little if any art history, because of his direct contact with living contemporary artists. As long as they were tastemakers, Rivers had a chance. Once the academic art historians influenced by Greenberg took over, Rivers was in trouble. Only the poets seemed to be a point of resistance to America's conservatism and its postwar suburban mentality.

What united Rivers to the New York School poets was an interest in everyday language. In Rivers' work this turned out to be the use of banal motifs like money and packages of cigarettes and cigars. Advertising and common objects had been used before as subjects for art. Both Gerald Murphy and Stuart Davis, for example, had been inspired by popular art. In the 1920s Davis painted a pack of Lucky Strike cigarettes, which Rivers made an emblem in the 1960s.

That Rivers should collaborate with his poet friends was only natural. In Paris he had met

Rivers with Clarice Price Rivers
and Kenneth Koch with *New York
1950–60* in Rivers' New York
studio, 1961
(Rudolph Burckhardt)

Tatyana Grosman, who wanted to do *livres de luxe,* special editions of poetry illustrated by painters. When she set up her own print workshop in the United States in West Islip, Long Island, in 1957, the first artist she called was Larry Rivers. Not surprisingly he chose to work with O'Hara. Their collaboration, *Stones* (Pls. 14 and 15), a series of twelve lithographs, was made in 1957–59. It was the first project of the legendary Universal Limited Art Editions (ULAE). At the time Grosman insisted that great lithography could only be made in the traditional way, by working directly on heavy limestones. As Rivers later recalled, he and O'Hara thought of themselves as Matisse and Éluard working together in a dialogue of images and words. These early collaborative projects with poets incorporating text would lead in the 1960s to Rivers' use of stenciled lettering in his paintings.

After *Stones,* Kenneth Koch decided that he, too, should collaborate with Rivers. The result was *New York 1950–60.* At first they worked on paper

Opposite:
Frank O'Hara and Larry Rivers
working on *Stones,* 1958
(Hans Namuth)

and then on canvas. Koch would write a phrase and Rivers would respond with a drawing. Koch recalled the process: "On the canvas, I would write something down, like 'not cylinders,' and Larry, being literal-minded in a certain way, would draw a cylinder. I remember feeling slightly disappointed because I didn't want it to be literal. . . . I suppose I wanted him to be more like me, but *it* was better that he wasn't."[18] In 1951 Rivers did a linocut print for the cover of a publication of Koch's *A Christmas Play*, which was typical of his interaction with writers.

By the time he began to collaborate with poets, Rivers, one suspects, was quite conscious of imitating his hero Picasso's ploy of involving his audience in his life, especially the soap opera of his sex life, which was sure to interest a public with no knowledge of art. The idea that representation gave artists a chance to, as Rauschenberg put it, "act in the gap between art and life" was enthusiastically embraced by Rivers, who has, as many including

Berdie, seated, posing for Rivers,
Southampton, 1954

himself have observed, an exaggerated need for
attention. If Picasso had the need and used it to his
advantage, dragging the public into the sordidness
of his personal life, then Rivers could do the same.

THE LIFE OF THE PARTY

*So if I have inherited natural bad taste it is at least
compounded with an obnoxious sense of who I am.*
— LARRY RIVERS, 1961 [19]

In his memoir, *The Party's Over Now,* John Gruen
gives an account of the high jinks that made the
Hamptons a paradise in the 1950s. The romantic
atmosphere of picnics on the beach and the avail-
ability of cheap housing made it the last true
bohemia. The social life consisted of house parties,
with friends casually dropping by, eating in because
there was no money to eat out. There were a few

mansions belonging to staid socialites, but for the
most part the "bonnikers," as the locals were
referred to because they lived near Akabonic Creek,
were the artists' neighbors.

In May 1953, disgusted with the reception of his
work and his life in general, Rivers gave his Manhattan loft to painter Howard Kanovitz. By this time
he had settled into an unusual domestic ménage
that included his sons, Joseph and Steven, and his
former mother-in-law, Bertha Burger, whom he
immortalized as the sagging Rubensesque Berdie in
his nude portraits of the older woman. With her aid
a desolate Rivers rented a house in Southampton for
$85 a month, which he paid for by selling an occa-
sional work, teaching art, and trucking furniture
into New York. His studio was in the garage.

In Southampton, Rivers began to make sculpture. Dealer Leo Castelli encouraged his efforts at
assemblage, commissioning a standing figure for
his East Hampton garden. In 1954 Rivers had his

Artist group portrait,
Southampton, ca. 1963

first exhibition of sculptures, at the Stable Gallery, New York. Poet William Berkson later wrote of the origins of Rivers' metal sculptures, like the 1957 *Iron Maiden,* considering them to be indebted to Julio Gonzalez, an artist Rivers claimed to admire. It was the moment of assemblage, and Rivers' figurative experiments deserve more attention than they have had. According to Berkson, "The steel for *Iron Maiden* came from the fenders of a Ford. . . . Part of the strangeness of this piece lies in the fact that it started out as a male figure for which the model was the painter Howard Kanovitz. As it is, the head is a neuter mask, the breasts grafted onto the torso. At first glance, it looked like a robot blasted from all sides by ray guns."[20]

By the time he moved to Southampton, Rivers had been thoroughly integrated not only into the Manhattan art world but also into the milieu of the Hamptons, where art and literature brushed shoulders. Beginning in the 1940s, it became the home

of the leading lights of the New York School, including Pollock, Krasner, and de Kooning. Photographers Hans Namuth and Rudolph Burckhardt – whose underground movie *Mounting Tension* (1950) included Rivers in its cast – documented the art world. Critic Harold Rosenberg held court, and those who did not have houses there, like John Bernard Myers, came to visit for weekends. In the circles within circles of the social life of the artists, there was a group of figurative painters whose guru was the poet and critic Fairfield Porter.

A regular contributor to *ARTnews,* Porter was a fine writer as well as a painter. His moving 1952 seated portrait of Rivers with his wrists bandaged after an attempted suicide gives one a sense of Rivers' desperate state of mind in his late twenties as he vacillated between music, art, and poetry, stumbling from disastrous liaison to liaison, never really understanding what went wrong. As a painter, Porter had developed a skillful interpretation of

Fairfield Porter
Portrait of Larry Rivers, 1952
Oil on canvas
50 x 30 in.
Colby College Museum of Art,
Maine
Purchase from the Jere Abbott
Acquisitions Fund

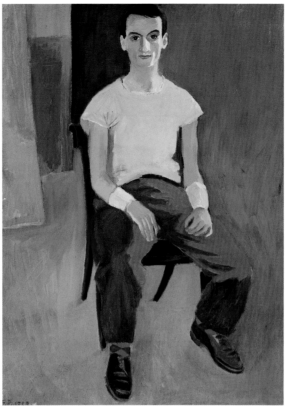

Matisse that also drew on American sources like Winslow Homer and Edward Hopper. Porter's intimate circle included the still-underestimated landscape painter Rackstraw Downs, Robert Dash, John Gruen's wife, Jane Wilson, as well as Grace Hartigan and Jane Freilicher, who chose to remain easel painters and intimists.

When Rivers decided to move to the country, Porter gave him the use of his barn as a studio where he could paint bigger pictures than in his garage. In the summer the area bustled with tourists and visitors from the city, but out of season the little resort was a quiet rural retreat that offered ideal working conditions. Rivers lived full-time in Southampton from 1953 through the fall of 1957. There he continued to develop and refine the style of painterly realism that had lines floating on surfaces that were sometimes patchy and sometimes atmospheric in the sense that Arshile Gorky, an artist Rivers much admired, combined a surrealist sense of indeterminate space with linear inflection. However, unlike Gorky, who invented a vocabulary

of organic forms, Rivers interpreted what he saw around him in paintings and drawings at that point still made from life.

Rivers insisted that his sitters pose nude. Among the large-scale works of the period are portraits of O'Hara, Rivers' sons and his estranged wife, who would show up from time to time, and of course the portraits of Berdie, at the time a woman in her sixties. His reasoning was that he was trying to learn how to paint nudes like the old masters. "Géricault painted a male nude perhaps two feet tall. I painted one eight feet high," he explained. "I felt competitive and wanted to prove myself as good, if not better, on their own terms. I wanted to paint flesh as pink sienna and gorgeous as anything done. I think I fell somewhere about a mile from what I wanted and tried to make up for the failure by size and number. You must love to imitate, but it is not enough."[21] The chutzpah to challenge the masters of past time on their own turf was matched only by the audacity of painting his friends, relatives, and himself nude.

Able to concentrate on his painting and undistracted (for once) by the lures of the big city, he made substantial strides in creating a style that occupied a fulcrum point between abstraction and representation without ever fulfilling the doctrines of either. In Southampton as in Manhattan he maintained a lifestyle centered on close friends – mainly poets – and family, who drifted in and out of a ménage as loosely constructed as the fluctuating space in the works he was painting. With so many free models around, these tended to be portraits. During this period he developed the mature style for which he is known, which interweaves linear drawing with patches of color set in an ambiguous, airy, lightly brushed ground.

We know how Rivers worked from the descrip-

The Studio, 1956
Oil on canvas
82½ x 193½ in.
The Minneapolis Institute of Arts,
Minnesota
The John R. Vanderlip Fund

tion given by his friend Fairfield Porter. For an important painting Rivers made many preliminary drawings of both the entire figure and details. He transferred the finished drawing to a canvas, wiping off excess color with rags soaked in turpentine. Rivers made no effort to disguise the alterations and adjustments of various elements of the composition, preferring to emphasize the process of constant revision through which his imagery developed. He worked from studies of the full pose and various details. *Pentimenti* are not only left visible but encouraged by the painter. They serve as reminders that the figures have a past and also as a general reference to the layers of memory encrusted in the artist's interpretation of his subject. Rivers transforms Cézanne's doubt into a cinematic shifting that recalls the panoramic movement of the movie camera traveling in space. As he depicts them in different places and positions, his figures have a past and a future, not merely a present. Thus they run totally against the aesthetic of the moment, which was the instant impact of holistic "one-shot" images that are immediately perceived because they have no detail or background.

"These paintings consist of the faint remains of all the things that I did not want, that the whole

canvas wouldn't give up no matter how much I scrubbed, scraped or merged," he told Porter, "so in a way, all of it grows out of an abundance of dissatisfactions." Porter wrote that "for Rivers drawing is the most important part of the painting, to which everything else is subservient and dependent."[22]

The Studio was painted in 1956 in Porter's barn. It does not include a self-portrait, which is the focus of Courbet's *Atelier,* but like Courbet's "real allegory" it is an immense tableau, more than sixteen feet long, and includes portraits of Rivers' family and friends. Rivers' ambitious painting, based on previous studies and arduous observation, marks his creation of a personal style reminiscent of the way the movie camera records images with swift horizontal pans. Figures are not seen in consecutive motion photographs, but rather in different positions simultaneously. There is an assurance in the drawing and a new, fresh pastel rococo palette. The traces of the process of painting the picture are intentionally left visible, and figures and objects are only partially indicated by linear depiction over fluid washes of pale color.

Parts of the canvas are left bare in the same way that Cézanne's late works are considered *non finito,* belying any type of volumetric reading. It is as if the

Rivers with Helen Frankenthaler
(left) and Tom and Audrey Hess

canvas is just another page covered with drawings.
The black dancer leaping through space reminds us
of Rivers' involvement in dance through his friendship with critic Edwin Denby and choreographer
Merce Cunningham, whose portrait he painted in
old age after the glamour of youth was gone. However, although Rivers depicts physical movement,
he does so with the hand as opposed to putting his
whole body into the record of the gesture of the
arm, the trademark of action painting.

The amorphous space that Rivers, surer of his
hand, was now creating, was diaphanous and indeterminate like that of Baziotes and Gorky, artists
for whom he had immense admiration. His pigment
now is more dilute and liquid. There are drifting
patches of color, and the canvas is treated like a
watercolor drawing. The coincidence between
Rivers' development of this technique and the technique of the stained color field painters like Rivers'
friend Helen Frankenthaler is noticeable and
reflects Pollock's treatment of the canvas support
as porous. The figures depicted sometimes in
various poses seem evanescent rather than solid,
sometimes dreamlike in the way they appear
and disappear.

In 1955 Rivers painted a *Double Portrait of
Berdie* (Pl. 10) using techniques derived from the
academic digressions of the previous year – illu-
sionistic space, fully modeled volumes, significant
detail, and psychological insight into his subject.
The painting was included in a new talent exhibition at Eleanor Ward's Stable Gallery in 1955, chosen by Thomas B. Hess, editor of *ARTnews* and a
staunch Rivers supporter. Leo Steinberg considered
the artists in the exhibition, who included Nell
Blaine, Michael Goldberg, Gandie Brodie, Joan
Mitchell, and Robert Rauschenberg (at the time
working as the janitor of the gallery), as essentially
the heirs of Hans Hofmann, whose styles pointed to
"an unruly slang, not a grammar of painting . . . a
passionate involvement in a moment of crisis, the
involvement repeating itself in each separate, rule-
breaking work." He had good words for many of the
second-generation New York School painters, but
he dismissed Rauschenberg as an entertaining
lightweight and he venomously attacked Rivers.[23]

Steinberg smashed Rauschenberg as the Eulen-
siegel of his day, "with his combines of elaborated
whimsy, glue and chic, predicting they would steal
the show (they didn't)." He had even more unkind
words for Rivers:

*We come at last to the open puzzle of Larry Rivers,
a painter who has thrown off the immediate influence of his preceptor Hofmann to undergo the teach-
ings of a previous century. He is one of the few
contemporary New York painters who take no pride
in displaying the discontinuous brushstroke as an
example of a unique personal rhythm. Instead of
painting from the shoulder, he makes his strokes fuse
into planes and volumes, quite in the manner of the
masters. Rather than submit things to style, he
affects to submit his style to the things represented.*

His huge and most recent Double Nude Portrait of Birdie *is at first sight a piece of downright realism in terms that everyone can understand.*[24]

Steinberg admits that "Rivers paints with intelligence and skill, since his paint surface gives off a seductive charm, and since he courts comparison with masters of past time, his work merits analysis."[25] However, he then spends the rest of a lengthy article ripping Rivers apart because although he dares to use old master technique, he flattens space and contradicts any illusion of depth created. These contradictions, however, are what permit Rivers to reconcile modernist spatial concerns with representation. "We are therefore confronted neither by a single moment, nor a single space, nor a single presence; and what we get accords neither with the ways of nature, nor with the needs of symbol, but solely with the vagaries of art."[26]

He berates Rivers because his modeling is not convincing, unaware that this precisely is the point, the reason we know this is artifice intentionally unconvincing as illusion. Steinberg writes admiringly, "Observe that his painting improves as you approach, and vice versa. An eye or mouth looks best studied point-blank. At close range one can share Rivers' pleasure in discovering anew how the upper lid of an aging eye surf-dives under a fold of skin; or, at the other end, how the seesawing of the leading edge of a toenail defines that toe's rotation on a foreshortened horizontal axis." Then he complains, "The forms weaken as one lets the eye take in a larger field. Then the near, shadowed side of a figure (the bright side for Rivers is usually the less accessible) becomes a formless and colorless patch. . . . Between the figure on the left and the rear wall I find only a suffocating airlessness as if the picture has been flat conceived, and then tried

to belie itself."[27] Finally, someone understood what Rivers was doing – and hated him for his betrayal of realism when he clearly was capable of completing the illusion.

Steinberg's diatribe notwithstanding, in 1956 Rivers was included in the prestigious series of exhibitions of new American art organized by Dorothy Miller for the Museum of Modern Art. In the *12 Americans* catalog Rivers commented on his tendency to meander "disregarding what others do, feel or think, my work at moments seems an attempt to solidify my identity with the great painters."[28]

The following year he found fortune not as an artist but as a TV quiz show participant who won $32,000 on *The $64,000 Question.* It was a large sum at the time, so when Berdie died, in 1957, Rivers could afford to move back to Manhattan with his sons. And in any event, it was time. Pollock had died in a car crash the previous summer, and tourists were filling the beaches and back roads where he died.

Rivers continued to summer in Southampton, where he still has a house. He usually played jazz in the local clubs as well as painted. In the Hamptons he made a point of finding Ivy League girls who became his models. Molly Adams, a WASP socialite, was, according to Rivers, his first real "girl friend." Molly was soon to be replaced by another college girl waiting tables, Maxine Groffsky. Legend had it that she was the inspiration for Brenda Patamkin, the New Jersey Jewish princess who was the heroine of Philip Roth's first novel, *Goodbye, Columbus.* Rivers began to draw Maxine as regularly as Picasso sketched Fernande. Then Maxine moved to Paris, where, according to Ernest Hemingway, good Americans go when they die.

I have a bad arm and am not interested in the art of holding up mirrors. Perhaps you will see Camel cigarettes or French money differently after looking at my paintings, but what's so marvelous about that? — LARRY RIVERS, 1963[29]

The 1950s were a decade of portraits and interiors, intimate scenes from the home life of the artist. From 1960 on, popular and commercial images became a major subject for Rivers. He presented them not in the hard-edge graphic style of the pop artists, but instead he perversely painted them with atmospheric effects, as if they were *plein air* studies. In response to the changing aesthetic that rejected the spontaneity and painterliness of action painting as well as figure-ground relationships as relics of the dead European tradition, in 1959 Rivers painted *Cedar Bar Menu I.* The painting duplicated the daily menu, filling the entire canvas with its handwritten image of the day's specials. When the original was lost, he painted a second version in 1960.

Shortly after, he turned his attention to playing cards and cigarette packaging in the painting *Pink Tareyton.* Rivers explained his fascination with such new still life subject matter: "If I am moved to work from these products," he told the audience of the symposium "Mass Culture and the Artist" in 1963, "it's for what I can take from them for my ideas of a work of art." He claimed that what interested him about advertising and packaging was "its flatness . . . the reduced conflict between what you are looking at and what you end up with on your canvas."[30]

Much as he might claim to be deaf to criticism, Greenberg's mantra of flatness as the fundamental characteristic of avant-garde painting was getting to Rivers, at least on some level if not actually consciously. Generally, he responded to things instinctively rather than programmatically, but when something of real note was happening, he was not asleep – as much as he might pretend to be detached from the aesthetic concerns of the art world. Like Johns' flags and targets, the logos on cigarette packages and cigar boxes were ready-made images, instantly recognizable as flat by definition. However, Rivers' interpretation of these images in a painterly style highlighting his skill as a draftsman makes the point that his paintings are unique, hand-painted originals, not to be confused with photographs or reproductions.

Artists elsewhere were also engaging this subject matter. In London, Richard Smith was painting images taken from advertisements and films and the dancing cigarette packs seen on television. Also using such images were the new realists in Paris, to which Rivers would soon travel.

Once Berdie was gone, Rivers engaged a young Welsh au pair, Clarice Price, to take care of Steven, who was still at home. Clarice was beautiful, voluptuous, funny, and Larry's equal in energy, brilliance, and capacity to scandalize. But she was also a homebody, a good cook, and extremely tolerant. Since Clarice was always home, she became not only the artist's wife but also his model. For six years, until Clarice finally threw Larry out of their Central Park West apartment because of the chaos he created, Rivers would have a domestic situation that gave him stability and (relative) peace of mind.

After their wedding in London in 1961, they continued on to Paris, where they stayed until the summer of 1962. They rented a studio in the Impasse Ronsin (near Brancusi's studio), a neighborhood that was having its last moments of

Cedar Bar Menu I, 1959
Oil on canvas
47½ x 35 in.
Private Collection

Niki de Saint-Phalle

Rivers at Tinguely's *La Forêt*,
ca. 1977

bohemian glory, its alleys filled with trash and assorted debris. It was a perfect place for Rivers to accumulate junk, gossip with his neighbors, and have parties.

Rivers had recently shown his welded sculpture in New York and was anxious to collaborate with Jean Tinguely, who was noted for his kinetic works. Tinguely and his future wife, Niki de Saint-Phalle, were part of the new realist group, which also included French pop artists Martial Raysse and Arman. Their champion was Pierre Restany, who organized an exhibition of their work for Sidney Janis in 1962 in New York. George Segal, who had recently joined the gallery, was included as was Rivers. The historic show is remembered as the official launching pad for pop art.

Probably because he and Clarice were trying to learn French (a hopeless task for both of them), Rivers began to paint the *Vocabulary Lessons* series. He also painted the portraits of his wife providing the French words for the features in stenciled letters. The lettering, which Johns had borrowed from the cubists, accentuated the flatness Rivers was now pursuing. The contrast between image and text as well as the combination of freehand and mechanical drawing required both reading and looking to be assimilated. In *Parts of the Body: French Vocabulary Lesson,* a series based on nude figure studies of Clarice, he also used stenciled lettering as a tautological reference.

In *Parts of the Body,* along with his drawings from life Rivers also incorporated images taken from correspondence-course drawing manuals of the human figure. He must by then have been aware of Lichtenstein's diagram of the portrait of Mme. Cézanne as well as Warhol's *Paint by Numbers,* which denied the individual subjectivity of the hand. Rivers' response was to draw the human body by hand and match his observation from life against the mechanical system that was supposed to make it possible for anyone to draw.

When he returned to New York, these dissections and recombinations of figure drawings found their three-dimensional equivalent in assembled sculptures. He also painted cigarette packages – Disque Bleu, Gauloises, Gitanes, and Camels – and he perversely depicted these flat images as shaded and spatial. The contradiction between what the

Parts of the Body: French Vocabulary Lesson, 1961–62
Oil on canvas
72 x 48 in.
Private Collection

*French Vocabulary Lesson, 1978
(after Parts of the Face: French
Vocabulary Lesson, 1961–62)*
Acrylic, pencil, and colored pencil
on paper
30½ x 24½ in.
Marlborough Gallery, New York

mind knows from experience and what the eye sees creates a tension that is difficult to resolve and somewhat maddening to perceive. Rivers found currency another worthy subject, possibly in response to Warhol's silk-screened two-dollar bill. But rather than enlarge and duplicate a photographed original, Rivers reclaims the uniqueness of his subject by painting the French franc with the same loving attention he paid to his wife's body.

When Rivers turned his attention to cigar boxes, he painted not a portrait of Daniel Webster but a portrait of the lid of a cigar box on which Webster's image appears. In a typically bizarre Rivers interpretation, he painted his subject surrounded by

a garland of fairy-tale pink roses in the 1961 *Webster Flowers,* which Ashbery compared to a Tiepolo. The *Webster Cigar Box* drawings and painting were shown in the spring of 1962 at the Galerie Rive Droite in Paris and then at Gimpel Fils Gallery in London.

In a sense we can see the paintings Rivers executed in Paris as a response to the static, dehumanizing properties of pop art. If Warhol insisted that his portraits were his still lifes, Rivers would manage to turn his still lifes into portraits, full of the breath of life. Given the amount of time cigar box lids occupied his attention, it is likely that Rivers heard the story of how Serusier came back from Pont Aven with a painting on the lid of a cigar box, saying that before a painting was a woman, a tree, or a sunset, it was colored patches on a flat surface.

In 1963 Rivers made a free copy of David's *Napoleon* in the National Gallery, Washington (see page 72). The diminutive, mincing emperor looks less like a colonial conqueror than he does like Marlon Brando playing Napoleon in the trashy film *Désirée.* Rivers titled his smug, pigeon-chested Napoleon *The Greatest Homosexual* (Pl. 32).

The painting is masterfully executed, with areas of bravura painting that would leave Sargent and Sorolla breathless. It is filled with contradictions, however. Patches of abstract color are interwoven with drawing and collaged elements. Contours give out just where they should convince one of the solidity of the figure. Modeling is detached from volume and floats around with a life of its own, quite independent of its normal job of suggesting the third dimension. As an image it is unforgettable. As a criticism of French colonialism, it was unforgivable.

Larry and Clarice Rivers with
Dutch Masters and Cigars II,
1963

I AM A MOVIE CAMERA

*In the past you could walk right up to a painting
if you were attracted, and the nearer you got the
more intimate you felt with the work. There was
something to examine close up. Today it doesn't
make any difference how close you get, you're still
just as far away as you were. There's nothing to
learn from detail. Paintings are done close up. But
today their impact is at a distance — the kind of
painting that looks the same thirty feet away as it
does at five feet.* — LARRY RIVERS, 1959 [31]

When Larry and Clarice returned to New York in
July 1962, he set to work on a series of sculptures

using window display mannequins sprouting metal
equivalents of the descriptive lines in the vocabulary lesson paintings. Another cigar box lid caught
his eye and set him painting the *Dutch Masters*
series. Nothing of course could match the cliché of
a reproduction of the hackneyed old Dutch master
image of Rembrandt's masterpiece *The Syndics of
the Clothmakers' Guild.* Emblazoned and embossed
on the lid of the cigar box of the brand called Dutch
Masters, it is the quintessential emblem of the
degradation of the high art of museums into low
reproductions of mass advertising. A second large
version, *Dutch Masters and Cigars II* (Pl. 31),
transferred the image to the canvas through silk-
screening, a printmaking technique that Warhol,
Rauschenberg, and Johns were all using in their
paintings.

The early 1960s were busy and productive years
for Rivers. Clarice was a stabilizing influence in
every way. Now he could show at a big-time Fifty-
seventh Street gallery, the Marlborough, which
could afford to promote his work. Suddenly the
beatnik holy terror began to look like a respectable
family man, which convinced patrons he could be
trusted with large-scale (and high-paying) public
commissions.

In 1963 he was commissioned to create a billboard for the First New York Film Festival at Lincoln Center. Rivers had to shift gears to conceive
on a very large public scale when at heart he was an
intimist. The result reveals ambivalence regarding
technology and reproduction and his nostalgia for
the early creative years of filmmaking, before com-
mercialism took over. If Christopher Isherwood
thought of himself as a camera in Berlin, Rivers
began to see his life and times with the eye of a filmmaker extending the still frame of collage to the
free association of montage, which in the mind

Billboard for the First New York Film Festival, 1963
Oil and charcoal on linen
114 x 286 in.
Hirshhorn Museum and Sculpture
Garden, Smithsonian Institution,
Washington, D.C.
Gift of the Joseph P. Hirshhorn
Foundation, 1966

combines images to create a third thing, the emotion their juxtaposition in time evokes.

There is always intention in Rivers' work, although it may not always be entirely conscious. Between John Myers and the poets, he had become an expert at stream-of-consciousness free association. The film festival billboard has references to the honky-tonk of neon, but its references to Hollywood are taken from vintage photos of silent film stars like Rudolph Valentino. The maquette caught the eye of Joseph Hirshhorn, and the eccentric multimillionaire collector, who became a close friend, bought it.

Rivers' family was growing – Gwynne was born in 1964 – as was his international reputation. In London, the Tate Gallery gave an exhibition of his sculptures done in the previous decade, ones that had not been particularly noticed or appreciated in the United States. He was also invited to be in *Docu-*

menta III in Kassel, Germany. In New York he continued painting the themes he invented in Paris. His swishy Napoleon and the travesty of Ingres's portrait of Mlle. Rivière were included in his 1964 show at Gimpel Fils in London. Norbert Lynton, who reviewed the exhibition, observed that "Rivers certainly takes the classicist's views of color as an added ornament to a design, which is the true carrier of expression and meaning." [32] Lynton claimed that Rivers elevated the sketch to monumental proportions – the same argument used by the academics against the impressionists – apparently because smaller works showing squared-up portions to be transferred were also included.

Squaring up from and enlarging a preliminary drawing was indeed the way a preliminary sketch was transformed into a finished painting. Rivers' decision to leave the penciled grid visible in the drawing was a self-conscious allusion to academic practice at the same time that he was parodying it. For a change, the joke went over like a lead balloon. Nevertheless, Lynton congratulated Rivers for his "lightness of tone . . . dexterity, wit, and entertainment . . . that lingers a long time and gradually reveals an underlying seriousness."[33]

THE PAINTER OF HISTORY

I am bothered by . . . so-called "pure" painting. Its specific demand for non-association is similar to the nineteenth century with its insistence on the proper association. Certain painters will not allow a recognizable image in their work (or anyone else's), just as the nineteenth century scored a painter who didn't make the image recognizable. Today, the figure is the hardest thing in the world to do. If it doesn't turn into some sort of cornball realism, it becomes anecdotal, it seems. Today, knowing the odds against you, the figure seems a stupid choice. But if the problem is one of choosing between being bored and being challenged, having to do the difficult, I'll take the latter.

— LARRY RIVERS, 1959[34]

In 1965 Sam Hunter organized Rivers' first comprehensive retrospective at the Rose Art Museum at Brandeis University, near Boston; the exhibit traveled to the Pasadena Museum, the Jewish Museum, the Detroit Institute of Arts, and the Minneapolis Institute of Arts. The success or the failure, or just the notoriety perhaps, brought him more work as a set designer, this time for the high-art Metropolitan Opera sets and costumes of Stravinsky's *Oedipus Rex.* The large-scale theatrical enterprise prepared him for the series of historic panoramas that were to occupy him for the next decade. For the New

York appearance of the retrospective, Rivers wanted to put the New York art world on edge with a work so big and ambitious it could not be ignored.

It was *The History of the Russian Revolution from Marx to Mayakovsky* (Pl. 33), a monumental, three-dimensional relief construction of epic narrative shown at the Jewish Museum in the fall of 1965. It is a huge, dizzying, mixed-media assemblage painting of events based on photographs, reproductions used as models for freehand painting, three-dimensional cutout figures, stenciled lettering, and real objects. The effect was like that of nineteenth-century dioramas, which rolled past the astonished audience caught up in the technical brilliance of the artist. The broad horizontal format of the multipart work was reminiscent of the panoramic view of CinemaScope. With its wealth of visual detail and images, it was not a feast but an orgy for the eye.

The History of the Russian Revolution was reproduced in a double-page spread in *Time* magazine, where Hirshhorn apparently first saw it. Rivers understood that the general public looked at art through reproductions in books and magazines and took that into consideration. However, rather than make paintings that looked like reproductions in the style of pop art, he chose like Johns to make obviously hand-painted originals based on reproductions and prints. Hirshhorn was determined to have the major work for his new museum in Washington, D.C. He promised Rivers every artist's dream – his own room. Hirshhorn demanded a bargain basement price, but finally Rivers decided the immense work would be better off even in the museum's cellar than in his studio.

In his memorial eulogy after Hirshhorn's death, in 1981, Rivers spoke philosophically: "What does make this world go round is a Talmudic question. No answers, just more questions." Rivers

Rivers assembling *The History of the Russian Revolution* for the Jewish Museum retrospective, 1965
(Basil Langton)

Rivers with (from right) Joe Hirshhorn, Olga Hirshhorn, Janet Solinger, and Steve Weil

Rivers holding daughter Emma
with Clarice Price Rivers holding
daughter Gwynne, on the S.S.
France, 1966

admitted that money was a lifetime worry and that
often Hirshhorn "walked out with some paintings,
but he was also buying dreams – mine and his. . . .
As I saw it, I was the artist in a drama about the
history of art. I made the appropriate gestures; I
played the role of connector from cave man artist up
through the present. You name them, I was
them." [35] Being the portrait painter of wealthy Jewish collectors did not endear Rivers to the snobby
art world. But Rivers was not a snob, and he had a
lot of people to support. Hirshhorn, of course, was
special because he was the first and the most out-
landish major private patron. His ambitions as a
collector matched Rivers' most megalomaniacal
fantasies: "If I'm to be recognized in this drama as
some kind of bohemian descendant of Michelangelo, Joe, all these years, was Lorenzo de Medici in
a business suit." [36]

Rivers clearly identified with Hirshhorn's
larger-than-life personality and his rags-to-riches
story. "In Joe's personal drama, in his fantastic
effort to bootstrap himself into eternity, he was the
star – a funny, peculiar, energetic, even a bumpy
one, full of costume changes: in society, a vaudevil-
lian; on the phone, a financial wizard and a vaude-
villian; in discussions of love, a father; at the dinner
table, a devourer of *latkas* [potato pancakes] – but a
star, and I played the supporting role." [37]

Rivers' affectionate portrait of Hirshhorn and
his wife, Olga, who sat for three days while Rivers
drew them from life, was painted only days before
Hirshhorn's death. His remarks reveal what moti-
vates Rivers as a portrait painter: "I was trying very
hard to satisfy both my idea of what makes a painting good, interesting, and meaningful, and what he
looks like, how he holds his body, sits tall or small in
a chair, and puts his arm around his wife." [38]

In 1966 Clarice and Larry's second daughter,

Emma, was born. This good news, however, was
shadowed by the tragedy of Frank O'Hara's acci-
dental death, which hit hard the whole of the New
York art world, in which the poet played such a key
role. It was a loss from which Rivers never really
recovered. The following winter he went to London,
sharing a studio with Howard Kanovitz. Then he
left for Africa with filmmaker Pierre Gaisseau to
make a television documentary commissioned by
NBC. By the time he returned to New York, Clarice
was demanding a separation.

Between his 1965 Jewish Museum retrospective
and 1970, Rivers did not have a major exhibition.
O'Hara's death left him without a best friend.
Clarice's rejection in 1967 left him without a family
or a home. Once again, he was a rootless bohemian
living in his studio. In 1968 Rivers returned with
Gaisseau to Africa to complete the documentary.
He sketched throughout the trip, which included
arrest and near execution in Lagos, Nigeria. These
sketches became the inspiration for *Africa II,* a
monumental summary of the current events in his
life. Freely associated images from mixed sources
surround the painted map of Africa; camels from

African Continent and Africans,
1970
Mixed media on canvas
45 x 36 in.
Menil Collection, Houston, Texas

the cigarette pack merge with the landscape to which they belong. A hallucinatory montage of jungle and swamp creatures, *Africa II* also includes brilliant passages of drawing in paint and atmospheric washes.

During the five years he had no gallery exhibitions, only one exhibition of drawings, Rivers was hardly idle. When he reemerged at the Marlborough Gallery in December 1970, it was with a major group of forty works done in the preceding five years. During this time he had executed three large-scale commissions: *The Boston Massacre* (1968) for the New England Merchants National Bank of Boston, *Forty Feet of Fashion* (1969) for the Smith Haven Mall, Lake Grove, Long Island, and the huge commission from the Menil Foundation based on three hundred years of black history, a work two years in the making that became known as *Some American History.* For each of these grand projects, he made drawings, sketches, maquettes, and all manner of preparatory materials that were finally seen in the finished mural assemblage paintings.

The mixed-media constructions in the Marlborough show were either fragments of these three

works or ones inspired by them. They included portraits of his friends Jim Dine, Frank O'Hara, and LeRoi Jones, who by that time was calling himself Imamu Amiri Baraka, as well as of Stravinsky, Lenin, and Daniel Webster. The show also included homages to Manet, David, and Ingres. There were reliefs and freestanding works incorporating drawings that were cut and folded into three-dimensional relief elements. He used not only canvas but plastic and wood. Not surprisingly, Hilton Kramer hammered the exhibition, calling it "jazzy, hip, decorative and a little nasty in its taste . . . the work of an artist who has liberated himself from all inhibition who dares to say or do anything in his art, but with fundamentally little or nothing to say." [39]

Kramer's was not the last word, however. Peter Frank thought the show reestablished Rivers as a powerful artist. "Rivers is . . . thrilling for his graceful, energetic line and structural sense," he wrote. [40] In the *New York Times,* Peter Schjeldahl, a longtime Rivers supporter, was particularly taken with four large sculptures titled *Shadow and Substance,* which were laminated and painted wood, life-sized, calendar-type nudes casting three-dimensional shadows. Identifying Rivers as "the only first-rank contemporary artist to regularly engage social and political themes," Schjeldahl sensed the artist's ambivalence: "He seems in expressing them at once hopeful and despairing . . . not sure whether the shock should be therapeutic or traumatic." [41] Rivers' commitment is finally not to the production of masterpieces (the idea of the masterpiece is in constant attendance) but rather to art as a kind of desperate adventure.

Kinko the Nymph Bringing Happy Tidings, 1974
Acrylic on canvas
78 x 108 in.
Art in Embassies,
U.S. Department of State,
Washington, D.C.

GOLDEN OLDIES

First of all, I've just been doing Oldies for a year and a half. And second, everybody does them and doesn't call them that. Look at Johns, Newman. . . . Their work is nothing else but Golden Oldies.
—LARRY RIVERS, 1979[42]

The 1970s were a disconnected series of trips around the world. In 1972 Rivers was in California, videotaping segments for an operatic adaptation of Kenneth Koch's poem "The Artist." Then he was off to Sweden and Africa again, to videotape what Peter Beard was photographing. For the bicentennial he painted a *Patriotic Stamps* series. And then he and George Segal traveled to Eastern Europe and Russia, at the invitation of the Union of Soviet Artists.

In 1974 paintings that Rivers had copied from Japanese erotic prints were shown at the Marlborough Gallery. He used the mechanical means of airbrush and stencils to help reproduce the look of woodblock printing. The biggest and most ambitious painting in the show, *Wedding Photo (Social Patterns),* was shown together with a detailed pencil drawing whose main purpose was to enable him to make stencils using tracing paper.

Three years later he began a series of paintings and drawings based on Rembrandt's *Polish Rider* (Frick Collection, New York). About the same time Rivers also began developing a new technique of carbon color projected imagery, an abstract arrangement of multicolored transfers taken from pieced-together sheets of carbon paper. In the *Color Carbon* series, he substituted preexisting images for his own original draftsmanship, embedded in a squared-off grid of prearranged colors.

In 1978 friend and collector Jeffrey Loria commissioned Rivers to paint the *Golden Oldies* series, part of which was shown at the ACA Galleries, New York. "What I'm doing," Rivers told Ashbery, "is taking subjects from my past and looking at them in the light of how I'm painting today." Ashbery explained that when asked about repetition in his work, Rivers came up with a two-part answer, more or less to the effect that (a) he wasn't repeating himself and (b) he was, but with a difference.[43]

THE CONTINUING INTEREST IN ABSTRACT ART

Only for the primitive and the semantically misinformed can enthusiasm for subject matter be the inspiration for painting. The roundness of a bright yellow grapefruit may make me happy for a few moments. Its juice may satisfy my thirst. I may find its genetic history engrossing, but as an artist what has meaning for me is the color I'm going to choose and where I'm going to put it on the surface and the way I put it there. What to choose and where to put it and how. — LARRY RIVERS, 1961[44]

For the next three years Rivers took up more intimate themes, which he generically titled, with his usual finger-in-your-face contradiction, *The Continuing Interest in Abstract Art.* Many of the images are family album snapshots that Rivers himself took. The theme of the artist observing himself is taken from the idea of *me voir me voyant,* the self-referentiality that André Gide describes. There is in fact much of Gide in Rivers' attitude. It was Gide after all who warned his reader: Do not understand me too quickly.

The 1980s for Rivers were in many ways a decade of stock-taking and reminiscence. In 1984, in *History of Matzoh: The Story of the Jews* (page 68), Rivers painted the chapters of Jewish traumas from Exodus to Herzl's creation of modern zionism. By now he had begun to feel that relief was necessary to

give greater impact to his detailed imagery, and so he has mounted the canvas on foamcore, a firmer version of Styrofoam that is easily cut to shape. In 1990 Rivers painted a specific scene from the Holocaust in *Four Seasons: Spring in the Forest of Birkenau* (Pl. 46), based on Manet's *Concert in the Tuileries.* Nothing in the painting, except perhaps its somber palette, announces the tragic fate of the assembled crowd.

During the 1990s Rivers quoted from the work of modern European masters in a series of foam relief sculptures covered with canvas and painted. He exhibited these at the Marlborough Gallery in May 1993. Ken Johnson wrote a largely sympathetic review in *Art in America:*

Soon to be 68, Larry Rivers has been making pictures of other old masters. Almost all the works in this recent show portray one of the fathers of modernism — Picasso, Matisse, Léger, Mondrian, and others — juxtaposed with one or more signature pieces of that artist's oeuvre. The pictures are made in relief: slabs of thick, sculpted foamboard are layered, carved and painted with brushy nonchalance to produce entertainingly theatrical composite images. As homages, they're rather ambiguous. The negligently facile, near-cartoonish painting, the gimmicky cutout relief and the presentation of the famous artist as a kind of Pop icon all hint at an ironic subtext.[45]

The series of *Art and the Artist* reliefs are essentially exaggeratedly shaped paintings. Areas and figures are cut out with a jigsaw and protrude forward and to the sides, dynamically breaking the frame and pushing the image into the viewers' space. The artists chosen are the heroes of modernism, clearly ancestor figures for Rivers. Rivers'

*Art and the Artist: Matisse and
"The Dance,"* **1992**
Oil on canvas mounted on
sculpted foamcore
77½ x 84 x 4 in.
Collection of the Artist

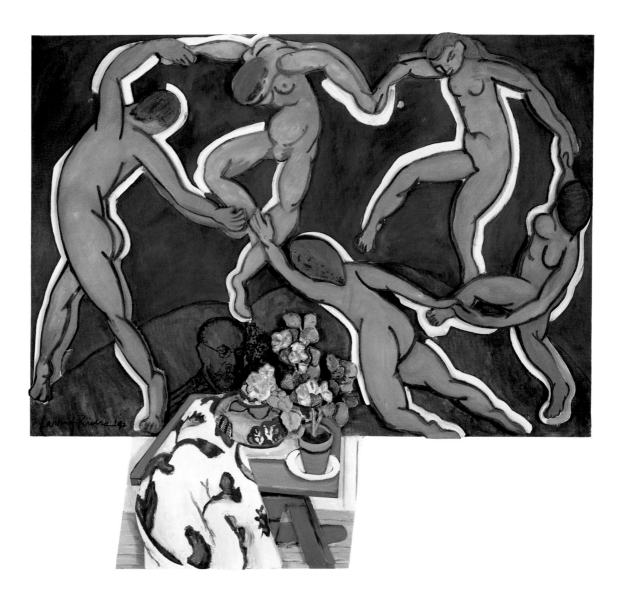

homages, however, are subversive of the originals.
Curiously, the artist to whom the greatest number
of works is devoted is not Picasso but Matisse. The
brilliant color of the series proves that at last Rivers
has mastered an aspect of painting that eluded him
most of his life, despite his studies with Hofmann.

In *Art and the Artist: Matisse and "The Dance,"*
Rivers depicts the painting on a much smaller scale

than the original. The photograph of Matisse is
combined with a reproduction of the famous fauve
painting and then drawn and painted by Rivers on
canvas, which is turned into a three-dimensional
relief and affixed to carved and sculpted foamcore.
Significantly, in the series of portraits of artists he
admires, Rivers includes Fred Astaire and Charlie
Chaplin. From all the artists he represents, we may

imagine that this thief of art has stolen something. His identification with performers, movie stars at that, reveals his wish to go beyond painting, not only to be as agile as Astaire and as funny as Chaplin the clown, but to bring to painting the fullness and drama, the spectacle and narrative, of film.

The question is always, Is he kidding? Is this Marcel Duchamp's "tongue in his cheek," or does Rivers really mean the schmaltz? The Holocaust images clearly mean it. There is no ambiguity about this tragedy, or about that of the slaves in his powerful *Auction, circa 1860* (Pl. 54). Here there is no mockery. Some of the most moving works are straight-on portraits of black musicians.

In the stylistic mix and match, we are caught in the confused whir of life documented in a visual diary that parallels the actual autobiography Rivers wrote with Arnold Weinstein. We are reminded of Picasso's claim that he was his sketchbook – *Je suis le cahier.* The adulteration and impurity of this mixture are no accident. Rivers intends to record not only his life, but the experience of his times, its confusion, posturing, desires, and disappointments. Rivers is a premature postmodernist appropriating images and incorporating words into his compositions.

As early as 1961, Rivers explained what he set out to do: "I want to emphasize that this is a false choice between a simple homey interest in things, or worldly, bad reemphasis on surface and style." He admonished himself not to take the easy way out: "The choice doesn't exist. Better we get rid of this dead body; perhaps we can resurrect something with a nastier, but more precise quality of meat on it."[46]

If one looks at Rivers' lifework as a piece, one finds threads of continuity, in subject matter, content, and style. From oil paints, acrylic, and metal to plastic, electric lights, and foamcore, the artist's materials have always served to further the narrative or figurative intention of his art. Its iconography is drawn from his acknowledgment that the individual is conditioned by historical, social, and economic circumstance. His candor is not calculated. The works offend and seduce at the same time. His lexicon of image making and representation – whether drawn, painted, photographed, silk-screened, collaged, or cut out – refuses to take sides. The Rivers you see is the Rivers you get.

NOTES

1. Charles Baudelaire, "The Painter of Modern Life," trans. P. E. Charvet, in *Baudelaire: Selected Writings on Art and Artists* (Cambridge: Cambridge University Press, 1972), p. 394.

2. In the film *Art/Work/USA,* which includes videos made by Rivers in the 1970s of surviving WPA artists.

3. Frank O'Hara, *Art Chronicles 1954–1966* (New York: Braziller, 1975), p. 110.

4. Ibid.

5. John Bernard Myers, "The Terrible Larry Rivers," *Artform* 16, no. 2 (October 1977): 53.

6. Manny Farber, *The Nation* 173 (October 10, 1951): 313-14.

7. Ibid.

8. Ibid.

9. Fairfield Porter, review, *ARTnews* 52, no. 9 (January 1954): 66.

10. Stuart Preston, *New York Times,* December 14, 1952, sec. 2, p. 9.

11. Robert Goodnough, *ARTnews* 51, no. 8 (December 1952): 44.

12. O'Hara, *Art Chronicles,* p. 113.

13. Larry Rivers, interview with the author in the film *American Art: The Sixties* (Blackwood Productions, 1968).

14. Larry Rivers, "A Discussion of the Work of Larry Rivers," *ARTnews* 60, no. 1 (March 1961): 54.

15. O'Hara, *Art Chronicles,* pp. 107-8.

16. John Richardson, "Dada, Camp, and the Mode Called Pop," *Journal of Aesthetics and Art Criticism* (Summer 1966): 552.

17. Susan Sontag, "Notes on Camp," in *Against Interpretation* (New York: Farrar, Straus & Giroux, 1966), pp. 275-92.

18. Helen Harrison, "A Conversation with Kenneth Koch," in *Larry Rivers: Performing for the Family* (East Hampton, N.Y.: Guild Hall Museum, 1983), p. 9.

19. Rivers, "A Discussion," 46.

20. William Berkson, "The Sculpture of Larry Rivers," *Arts Magazine* 40, no. 1 (November 1965): 50.

21. O'Hara, *Art Chronicles,* p. 111.

22. Fairfield Porter, "Larry Rivers Paints a Picture: A Portrait of Berdie," *ARTnews* 52, no. 9 (January 1954): 58.

23. Leo Steinberg, "Month in Review: Contemporary Group of New York Painters at Stable Gallery," *Arts Magazine* 30 (January 1956): 48.

24. Ibid.

25. Ibid.

26. Ibid.

27. Ibid.

28. Dorothy Miller, ed., *12 Americans* (New York: Museum of Modern Art, 1956).

29. Symposium "Mass Culture and the Artist," Museum of Modern Art, New York, October 8, 1963.

30. Ibid.

31. O'Hara, *Art Chronicles,* p. 120.

32. Norbert Lynton, "London Letter," *Art International* 8, nos. 5-6 (June 1964): 73.

33. Ibid.

34. O'Hara, *Art Chronicles,* p. 119.

35. Memorial address, Hirshhorn Museum and Sculpture Garden, September 16, 1981.

36. Ibid.

37. Ibid.

38. Ibid.

39. Hilton Kramer, "Art: The Rivers View," *New York Times,* December 17, 1970.

40. Peter Frank, "Art Exhibitions," *Columbia Spectator,* January 8, 1971.

41. Peter Schjeldahl, "Larry Rivers: Achingly Erratic," *New York Times,* December 27, 1970.

42. John Ashbery, "Of Time and Rivers," *New York,* October 29, 1979: 93.

43. Ibid.

44. Rivers, "A Discussion," 45.

45. Ken Johnson, "Larry Rivers at Marlborough," *Art in America* 81, no. 5 (May 1993): 117.

46. Rivers, "A Discussion," p. 46.

Larry Rivers and His "Smorgasbord of the Recognizable"

JACQUELYN DAYS SERWER

"As far as I am concerned, *nothing* makes an invented shape

more moving or interesting than a recognizable one.

I can't put down on canvas what I can't see. I think of a picture

as a smorgasbord of the recognizable." — LARRY RIVERS, 1959[1]

Larry Rivers has shocked, scandalized,

titillated, and awed his audience for more than fifty years. A true

adventurer, he has chosen his own path in art as well as life, often

preferring risk over prudence in order to do things his way. Rivers poses

a question in the title of his 1992 autobiography, *What Did I Do?*

Happily for the reader, the answer is "almost everything." A son of

Russian immigrants, he grew up in the Bronx as Yitzroch Loiza (Irving)

Grossberg. He became a professional jazz musician in his late teens.

Later, as a painter, sculptor, poet, and filmmaker, he achieved a level of

sophistication to match that of the writers, poets, and playwrights who

became his closest friends. He also traveled and lived abroad – in Europe,

**Rivers with his wife Clarice,
Southampton, 1976**
(Hans Namuth)

Paris especially, and in Africa. Rivers has maintained to this day his existence as a Renaissance man, writing, playing the saxophone, and making art, all the while taking a rather impulsive, improvisational approach to these endeavors. His studio on New York's East Thirteenth Street, his primary residence for almost forty years, housed living quarters and a painting studio, as well as a performance space where Rivers rehearsed until recently with his jazz ensemble, the East Thirteenth Street Band.

For much of his career, observers and critics saw Rivers as a rebel deliberately swimming against the tide of prevailing movements for the sake of sensationalism and the thrill of challenging the status quo. By now we can see Rivers' rebellious moves as those of a true innovator whose once subversive ideas have become part of the accepted repertoire of contemporary art. Clichéd subject matter, whether cultural or commercial; the use of industrial techniques and materials; the inclusion of stenciled words and language fragments as key elements; complicated works consisting of constituent parts that blur the boundaries between traditional painting and sculpture and what we now call installation art; his appropriation of imagery and techniques from other artists; and the balance he maintains between formal concerns and narrative content all are characteristics taken for granted in the art of today. Rivers claims that "not one day of my life have I wasted in searching for the truth,"[2] but the value and validity of his art defy any credible challenge.

Rivers' brash demeanor and candid language suggest the street-smart hustler, devoid of empathy and sentiment. In reality, though, his persona could not be more different. He is a man whose every experience has contributed to his awareness and understanding of the outside world, and he has been able to mine those experiences to give his art unusual breadth in subject matter, social awareness, and technical sophistication. Who else would have chosen George Washington and his own mother-in-law as major subjects in the 1950s; foreign dictionaries, civil rights (as a white artist), and the Russian Revolution in the 1960s; Japanese coloring books and Manet's *Olympia* in the 1970s; the 6,000-year epic of the Jews and 3-D renditions of Fred Astaire in the 1980s; slavery as well as the history of American movies in several giant mixed-media canvases in the 1990s?

In the early 1990s an exhibition of Rivers' work entitled *Public and Private* toured the country.[3] The premise – that Rivers worked in both realms, yet the two in many cases converged – has always been true of Rivers' approach. His subjects and their execution almost always function on both levels, presenting on close examination a remarkable panorama of Rivers' life and art in three-dimensional, multimedia Technicolor. As Rivers put it: "I remember everything I know, even the most superficial things. And what comes out is in my canvases."[4] When we interpret Rivers' work this way, as a continuum of the private and the public, the subjects seem to fall largely into several rich categories: personal history, history and politics, the French connection, art and artists, and show business.

PERSONAL HISTORY. According to Rivers, "It's history that makes a person something."[5] Rivers has chronicled his personal history both explicitly and implicitly. In the works that reflect this theme, Rivers has produced portrait after portrait of close family members and friends, as well as mementoes of friendships, and works commemorating significant epochs in his life. During one period in the

1950s, when Rivers was living year-round in Southampton, New York, he made a drawing of everyone who came into his studio: "My drawings were like moments."[6] Despite what many would consider Rivers' rather bohemian lifestyle during most of his adult life – parades of girlfriends, offspring resulting from sequential relationships, periods of experimentation with drugs, relationships with members of both sexes – Rivers has maintained a steadfast devotion to his family and friends that would rival that in most conventional lifestyles. The many pictures linked to his private life testify to the stability of the personal connections that have shaped his life and art.

The first decade of these pictures – the many images of Bertha ("Berdie") Burger, his sons, several self-portraits, as well as portraits of his poet-friends in the 1950s – document Rivers' life at the time. Berdie, his most frequent sitter during this period, surely ranks as one of the most unusual

muses in the history of art. The mother of his estranged first wife, Augusta, Berdie was, according to Rivers, "a person of slightly substandard mentality with no conventional talent whose daily behavior was concerned only with satisfying everyone else's needs."[7] This predisposition to self-sacrifice made her the perfect grandmother to his two boys, Joseph and Steven, who lived with him rather than their mother, and the most patient of models for a myriad series of paintings, drawings, and sculptures.

Double Portrait of Berdie (1955; Pl. 10) constitutes the most famous, or "infamous," representation of Rivers' mother-in-law. By depicting with merciless detail progressive images of its subject, one seated and the other upright, and moving toward the viewer's space, Rivers broke all the acceptable rules for avant-garde art of the time. He points out, however, that even with such a realistic rendering of the subject, he created an "overall" treatment of the painting's surface,[8] a characteristic

stylistic approach. The paintings display his use of thinned pigment that flows across the canvas, leaving almost no tactile traces. The sculptures, however, have rough, deeply modeled surfaces, emphasizing the artist's hands-on process of creation. The small painted plaster of Berdie is particularly charming, since it shows both the highly worked surface characteristic of the sculpture and the delicate, painterly treatment associated with his works on canvas.

Several full-length portraits precede the representations of Berdie. *Self-Figure* (1953; Pl. 2), purchased for the Corcoran from its 1954 Biennial, shows Rivers in much the same pose and style as the figure of George Washington in his picture *Washington Crossing the Delaware* (1953; Pl. 3). Depicting himself one-eyed and surrounded by *pentimenti* marking alternate placements of the figure and its parts, Rivers achieved an imposing yet ephemeral, almost ghostly rendering on a monumental scale.

linking him, ironically, with the then-dominant abstract expressionist style. While some remarked on the audaciousness of such a jolt of reality in the midst of the abstract expressionists' universe, others focused on the work's anatomical disjunctions and the disconnect between "so clinical an eye for obnoxious detail" and the decorative treatment of the lyrical embellishments in the background. In his most pompous manner, critic Leo Steinberg pronounced it "a picture in which genuine nastiness couples with false charm."[9] According to Rivers, he executed at least twenty portraits of Berdie.[10] *Berdie with the American Flag* (1955; Pl. 13) shows Rivers in his other, more painterly mode, and the dramatic inclusion of the flag coincides with its prominence in Jasper Johns' work of about the same time.

Not all of the Berdie portraits were in paint. Rivers also executed several sculptures in bronze (Pls. 1 and 4) and in plaster (one extant in the artist's studio; Pl. 5) that demonstrate still another

Portrait of Frank O'Hara, 1953
Oil on canvas
54 x 40 in.
Marlborough Gallery, New York

Augusta, 1954
Oil on canvas
83 x 53 in.
Collection of the Artist

The treatment of the figure suggests the influence of one of Rivers' early idols, Willem de Kooning (1904–97), whose works from the late 1930s (such as *Seated Man,* opposite) Rivers describes as having "had the greatest effect" on him.[11] Rivers' only other self-portrait in the exhibition, *Me in a Rectangle* (1959; Pl. 16), marks an entirely different stage in his evolving style. In this painting Rivers himself serves as a motif for an almost totally abstract rendering in the flashy style of the most dramatic action painting of the period.

The full-length nude of poet and curator Frank O'Hara (1954; Pl. 6), described as "a champion stud in leather combat boots,"[12] is one of several Rivers portraits of this major art-world figure of the 1950s and 1960s. It belongs with the portrait *Augusta* (1954), set in the same basement location of the artist's house in Southampton. With these nudes Rivers challenged himself to meet the old masters on their own ground. O'Hara's portrait references a nude once attributed to Géricault

(A Nude Study) in the collection of the Metropolitan Museum of Art.[13] But it is also about Rivers' close connection to O'Hara, with whom he had both a sexual relationship and an intellectual bond that later resulted in many collaborations, the first of which, *Stones* (1957–59; Pls. 14 and 15), was a pioneering artist-poet project for the New York artists of his generation. A series of lithographs consisting of text by O'Hara and drawings by Rivers, *Stones* became Tatyana Grosman's pilot project for ULAE Press, afterward the leading print studio of prominent contemporary artists for the next several decades.[14]

The 25 Cent Summer Cap (1956; Pl. 12) commemorates another major friendship with a writer, playwright Kenneth Koch. Represented as young and carefree, in Rivers' soft, watercolor-quality rendering Koch could have been mistaken for one of Rivers' children. Instead, like O'Hara, he was an influential figure in the realm of New York's intellectuals, and he collaborated with Rivers on a number of projects – stream-of-consciousness encounters on

Modeling Begins Early,
1996–2001
Pastel on paper mounted on
wood
48 x 45½ in.
Collection of the Artist

Larry Rivers and Frank O'Hara
working on *Stones* in Rivers'
New York studio, 1958
(Hans Namuth)

canvas, where Koch improvised as Rivers painted. Rivers also illustrated books of Koch's poetry.[15]

Rivers' *Portrait of a Man* (1954; Pl. 7) depicts his first dealer, John Bernard Myers, another member of Rivers' inner circle of intense relationships in the late 1950s and 1960s. He represented Rivers at the Tibor de Nagy Gallery for some twelve years. When Rivers moved to the then Marlborough-Gerson Gallery,[16] Myers interrupted Rivers' first Marlborough opening with the delivery of a summons charging him with breach of contract as a result of his move to the more prestigious gallery.

The other portraits of family members testify to the unorthodox but harmonious household Rivers had established in Southampton following his move there in 1953. *The Family* (1954-55; Pl. 8), a boxy portrayal of a clothed Berdie posed with Rivers' nude sons, along with another painting, the charming tableau of son Steven in *Boy in Blue Denim (Portrait of Steven)* (1955; Pl. 9) suggest a close-

knit, if eccentric, set of family relationships. Rivers embellished the latter picture with such exquisite details as the upholstery of the too-large brocade chair on which Steven sits, the plaid of his rolled-up jeans cuffs, and the stripes and decorative arches of the room's interior – altogether a major effort in honor of his unusual ménage. *The Family,* almost like an old master "sacred conversation," the formulaic figure groups featuring the Madonna and saints, seems a bit stilted, but it is also rather moving and awkwardly tender. The spatial disjunctions represented by the overlapping rectangles pushing forward and backward show Rivers acknowledging the cubist-informed atmosphere of the abstract art being made around him.

The sculpture *Don't Fall* (1966; Pl. 35) marks a new epoch in Rivers' career and his private life. It shows his use of nontraditional materials – plastics, electrical components – and it depicts one of his two daughters by his second wife, Clarice, entering a bathtub. Its origin can be traced to "a color photograph advertising the traction and the safety features of a rubber bath mat."[17] In *The Continuing Interest in Abstract Art: From Photos of Gwynne and Emma Rivers* (1981; Pl. 40), both daughters are featured along with Rivers' father shortly before his death. As usual, Rivers' family pictures fail to resemble anyone else's home album – few fathers would be comfortable recording themselves in the act of painting a prepubescent daughter's vagina – but the painting does achieve its own dreamlike nostalgia for times past and innocence lost.

Studio Interior (1990-91; Pl. 49) and *Modeling Begins Early* (1996-2001) bring the professional and family epic toward the present. Rivers' classic artist's self-portrait in the studio includes a backdrop of recognizable earlier works as well as the current projects of the time. *Modeling Begins Early*

depicts Rivers' youngest offspring, Sam, whose mother is the painter Daria Deshuk. It is done in his 1990s style of crisper edges, yet it harks back to *Double Portrait of Berdie* in its juxtaposition of two sequential images of the same figure.

HISTORY AND POLITICS. Rivers has always been interested in history. He is also, according to Peter Schjeldhal, "the only first-rank contemporary artist to regularly engage social and political themes."[18] With his history painting *Washington Crossing the Delaware* (1953; Pl. 3),[19] Larry Rivers made his debut on the stage of New York's lively art scene, which was still coming to terms with its relatively new status as the contemporary art center of the Western world. The year before, Harold Rosenberg

had published his celebrated "The American Action Painters" in *ARTnews.*[20] The same year as Rivers' *Washington,* Jackson Pollock painted *Portrait and a Dream,* where figuration enlivened one side of a two-part composition. De Kooning showed his *Paintings on the Theme of the Woman* at the Sidney Janis Gallery, and Josef Albers produced another *Homage to the Square (In Wide Light).* Even with the reemergence of figurative elements in Pollock and de Kooning, no one could have anticipated Rivers' monumental homage to Emanuel Leutze's painting of the same subject in the Metropolitan Museum of Art, one of the kitschiest images in American art. In fact, the painting wasn't about Leutze at all. Rivers' *Washington* served as his declaration of war on the limitations of abstract expressionism and his proclamation of independence in the area of subject matter. Rivers employed another conceit related to art history by basing Washington's head on Leonardo's drawing of *An Old Man in Hell.* Rivers then "placed the Leonardo head on a half-invented, half Jacques-Louis David body."[21]

The thought process that culminated in Rivers' choice of the George Washington scene began with his reading of Leo Tolstoy's *War and Peace.* As Rivers put it, "By meshing Napoleon's invasion of Russia with contemporary life, Tolstoy set me on a course that produced *Washington Crossing the Delaware.* This work was going to take my style of painting, charcoal drawing and rag wiping, to a new height."[22] Rivers had earlier admitted that ambition and ego also played into his choice: "I was energetic and egomaniacal and, what is more important, cocky and angry enough at the time to want to do something no one in the New York art world doubted was disgusting, dead and absurd, rearrange the elements, and throw it at them with

Photograph of Rivers' great-uncle and his family, the basis for *Europe I*

cross-fertilize subjects with his personal life, Washington looks suspiciously like Rivers himself in his full-length *Self-Figure,* painted the same year. When Rivers commented on this self-portrait, he admitted that since he was tempted to continue with takeoffs on historical subjects he "could have easily been Lincoln at Gettysburg." [24]

Rivers chose several other war-related subjects in the 1950s and 1960s. *Europe I* (1956; Pl. 11) served as Rivers' statement on life in old world Jewish communities shortly after World War I, communities like the one from which his parents had emigrated. The image is based on a family photograph showing his great-uncle and cousins. Photographs, or at least the reproduction of two photographs in *Life* magazine, serve as the basis for the *Last Civil War Veteran* series as well. One appeared in the May 11, 1959, issue and the other January 11, 1960. In *The Last Civil War Veteran* (1961; Pl. 18), the sketchily painted, bedridden former soldier is flanked by both the Confederate and American flags set against a decorative, flowered wallpaper background. The cross of the Confederate flag is eerily slanted, reminiscent of the cross Christ carried on the road to Calvary in old master canvases.

In another version, *Dead and Dying Veteran* (1961; page 66), Rivers utilizes a double image, the veteran still alive and bedridden, framed by his uniform and both the Confederate and American flags; and the veteran dead, in state, and attended by a marine guard. The subtle juxtaposition and melding of the before and after scenes creates a kind of dreamlike sequence that suggests the subtle transition from one state to another, from one epoch to another, in the normal course of the cycle of life as well as the cycle of history. In both versions Rivers once again dipped his brush into the action

great confusion. Nothing could be dopier than a painting dedicated to a national cliché." [23]

The subject and its derivation struck the art world as odd enough, but Rivers' episodic vignettes of related scenes, the ghosts of lines and forms partially wiped out, and the representational imagery pressed eerily against the picture plane (General Washington's boat seems about to dump him forward out of the boat and into the viewer's space) startled and outraged some in the art world. It exhilarated others. As if to prove he could wield the same techniques as the avant-garde even if he chose to use them for a different end, Rivers' canvas displays a luscious, painterly surface worthy of any action painter. In keeping with Rivers' tendency to

Dead and Dying Veteran in Rivers retrospective at Jewish Museum, New York City, 1965

painter's cans, but unlike the earlier painting of Washington, the forms are broader and bolder, the colors brighter and more saturated, and the elegant drawing, though still ghostly, is more emphatic.

In Rivers' engaging repertoire of history paintings, the centerpiece is surely *The History of the Russian Revolution from Marx to Mayakovsky* (1965; Pl. 33). An epic work of room-size scale (approximately fourteen by thirty-two feet), it consists of more than seventy separate components, including paintings, found objects, Plexiglas panels, empty frames, a storm window, pipes, and a machine gun. As in the case of *Washington Crossing the Delaware,* the idea for the work came from Rivers' reading material: a biography of Leon Trotsky by Isaac Deutscher. The concept of a monumental work suited the challenge Rivers had set for himself in the spring of 1965. A major venue for his 1965 retrospective was the Jewish Museum in New York, and he needed something spectacular to impress an art world not always receptive to his accomplishments. Without a doubt, the unveiling of this ensemble piece at the New York venue

ensured the exhibition's popular and critical success. *New York Herald Tribune* reviewer Emily Genauer pronounced Rivers' Jewish Museum show the "most sensational exhibition in its history" (Robert Rauschenberg and Jasper Johns had had one-person shows at the Jewish Museum in 1963 and 1964, respectively), and spent most of her review discussing *The History of the Russian Revolution.*[25] She devoted a subsequent article entirely to this single work.[26]

Choosing a sweeping, panoramic approach, Rivers covers almost seven decades of players and events related to the revolution. Working from left to right, he begins with Marx and Engels, includes two of the czars, political figures like Lenin, Kerensky, Trotsky, and Stalin, writers such as Gorky and Mayakovsky, and ordinary peasants and workers. The story ends with the suicide of Mayakovsky, shown at his desk, holding a gun to his head, next to the text of his poem "The Worker Poet."[27] The rhythm of shapes and images, paintings on canvas mounted on wood panels; the relief components such as Gorky seated at his desk, protruding, in

Working photo of the *History of the Russian Revolution*, in Rivers' kitchen

perspective, into the viewers' space; and the elements added to the surface of the sumptuous garments worn by Czar Nicholas and Czarina Alexandra provide the viewer with a theatrical experience. Critic William Berkson described it as "a stage that has walked away with the play, the actors and the stage itself."[28]

The History of the Russian Revolution marked an important milestone for Rivers, coming as it did at the very end of the first fifteen years of his career, and in many ways it summarizes his achievements up to that time. It also relates to his personal history. His mother had emigrated from what was then Russia, shortly after the revolution, and her brother had been killed there by the communists.[29] His ability to evoke not just an event, but a phenomenon; the mix of styles ranging from the most detailed images based on historic photographs to the elaborate abstract expressionist riff on the panel devoted to Stalin; the combination of disparate materials cobbled together in an astonishingly fresh and lively manner; and the centrality of a narrative based on objective facts that happen to

coincide with his own heritage – all these give this work unusual depth and resonance. While it looks back, referencing earlier achievements, it also looks forward, containing many elements that presage Rivers' accomplishments to follow.

Rivers' practice of incorporating words into his compositions has continued to be a common characteristic of his approach to picture making in such works as *History of Matzoh: The Story of the Jews* (1983), *Primo Levi: Survivor* (1987), and the *History of Hollywood* series he began in the late 1990s (Pl. 58; also pages 82–84), as well as the portraits of poets and writers such as John Ashbery and Allen Ginsberg. Perhaps this tendency stems in part from the fact that a Rivers work often has its origins in a literary source. *Russian Revolution* also allowed him to perfect his storm window portraiture, a format first realized in a work depicting an artist friend, Jim Dine (1965; Pl. 34). The three-dimensional elements in the work (many of the portraits, especially, have wooden pieces attached to the flat surface) effectively bring texture and depth to the images. A version of this relief treatment can be seen in Rivers'

History of Matzoh: The Story of the Jews Part III, **1984**
Acrylic on canvas
116¼ x 180 in.
Private Collection, New York

more recent foamcore works. The often repeated description of Rivers' work as stylistically inconsistent over the course of his career fails to take into consideration the many aspects that have remained constant throughout five decades.

Since the 1980s, Rivers has demonstrated a strong interest in his Jewish history, especially the story of the Holocaust. In the late 1980s, he achieved a notable success with the three paintings, in addition to related drawings, depicting Primo Levi, the Italian author and Holocaust survivor. Painted on canvas that is then mounted on foamcore, a stiff material that can be cut to shape, each of the paintings represents a different aspect of Levi's experience of near death and survival in one of the Nazi death camps during World War II. *Primo Levi: Survivor* (1987; Pl. 44) shows Levi as an older man,

healthy and serene, with another image superimposed of a much younger Levi, in a striped concentration camp uniform, emotionally devastated and physically emaciated. Another of the paintings, *Periodic Table* (1987), pictures Levi in front of the ovens where the remains of the dead were destroyed, with chemicals used in the killing process casually scribbled across the surface. The third picture, *Witness* (1988), shows Levi in combination with fragments of the fences surrounding the camp and images of arriving children who soon lost their lives. Italian journalist Furio Colombo sees the Levi portraits as incarnations of Rivers himself: "I saw Primo Levi emerge in Rivers' paintings like an image from the artist's own memory, a loved experience of Rivers himself. Primo Levi, poet and Jew of another life, another time, another country, became – as in

Primo Levi: Periodic Table, 1987
Oil on canvas mounted on
sculpted foamcore
73 x 58½ x 4 in.
Collection La Stampa, Turin, Italy

Primo Levi: Witness, 1988
Oil on canvas mounted on
sculpted foamcore
75½ x 68 x 5 in.
Collection La Stampa, Turin, Italy

a séance-like experience (in the highest, most mysterious sense of the word, an 'artistic' experience) – Larry Rivers, and Rivers painted himself having become Primo Levi."[30]

Four Seasons: Spring in the Forest of Birkenau (1990; Pl. 46) addresses the tragedy of the Holocaust as well. In this painting, based on a photograph taken from *The Auschwitz Album,* a collection of photographs that survived the war years, what looks like normal families congregating in the woods actually turns out to be a group of Jews on their way to a concentration camp.[31] As Sam Hunter described it, Rivers "managed to transform the grim scene by association, through impressionist style, onto quite another historical stage, the Isle-de-France around 1880, evoking at the same time a quite antipathetic cultural context and milieu in the vaguely suggestive setting of a pastoral idyll."[32] As a

result of this matter-of-fact treatment, the truth of the real situation becomes even more disturbing.

In the same ironic mode Rivers tackled another emotionally wrenching subject in his 1990s works dealing with American slavery. *The Auction, circa 1860* (Pl. 54), the centerpiece of this group, presents a large panorama of a slave auction based on a nineteenth-century print, which Rivers recalls having seen accompanying a newspaper book review of Peter Kolchin's *American Slavery, 1619–1877.*[33] Set in Virginia, Rivers' monumental treatment of the scene shows small groups of white men chatting and socializing as the auction of a black man, woman, and baby takes place on a platform in the center of an indoor meeting room. Other black men are waiting their turn on the auction block, one having his eyes poked and examined, presumably by a prospective buyer. All appears routine and normal. The

Rivers in Paris, 1950

color – bright yellows, blues, and soft reds – adds to the perversely festive scene. Rivers' use of the foamcore support pushes the action out toward the viewer's space, establishing a discomforting intimacy. As in *Four Seasons,* the seemingly unremarkable character of the individuals and the event makes the evil taking place even more shocking.

The drawings Rivers did in conjunction with *The Auction* include images of slave life, black minstrels, and a version of his nude picture of jazz saxophonist Sonny Simmons, this time with minstrel musicians pictured on the wall behind and a written list of favorite minstrel songs flanking Sonny Simmons on both sides. "The real artistry of these drawings," one reviewer wrote, "is the way they seduce us into confronting a history and a reality that many would rather forget." [34]

THE FRENCH CONNECTION. Rivers made his first trip to Paris in 1950. By his own description he did very little painting but spent his time writing poetry and

taking language lessons. During the months there he immersed himself in French literature and art: "What I didn't see on walls I found in artbooks; and the first 'literature' I read . . . with a dictionary right next to my mattress on the floor, was Balzac, Flaubert, Stendhal. And Baudelaire, the poet with the black mistress, whom I finally discovered leaning against a wall in Courbet's *Studio* painting." [35]

In addition to Courbet, Rivers found himself drawn to Delacroix, Cézanne, and the modernists Matisse and Picasso. His encounter with Bonnard in the retrospective at the Museum of Modern Art in 1948 had already predisposed him to the Gallic tradition. Years later, when pressed to name a favorite painting he would like to own, he described Courbet's painting of a girl lying down with a bird on her hand (*Woman with a Parrot,* 1866). "Every time I saw the painting I almost cried." [36] Rivers later executed two major paintings inspired by other Courbet works: *The Burial* (1951; opposite) and *The Studio* (1956; page 35).

Rivers returned to Paris in 1958 and again for an extended sojourn from October 1961 to July 1962. Before leaving New York he had begun painting pictures drawn from playing cards, such as *Three Kings* (1960; Pl. 17), and other popular culture imagery, including cigarette packages and cigar boxes, which he first exhibited at the Tibor de Nagy Gallery. To offset the tendency of the critics to pigeonhole him as a pop artist just as that movement was beginning to be recognized, he added a painting based on an Ingres portrait he entitled *I Like Ingres, Too* (1961). Once in France his interest in such mundane subjects continued, resulting in his many paintings and drawings based on French money. In collaboration with his neighbor on Rue Ronsin in Paris, the Swiss artist Jean Tinguely, he created *The Friendship of America*

The Burial, 1951
Oil on canvas
69 ½ x 104 in.
Fort Wayne Museum of Art,
Indiana
Gift of the Gloria Vanderbilt
Purchase Fund
1958.12

and France (Kennedy and De Gaulle) (1961–62; repainted, 1970; Pl. 22), with portraits of the two leaders and cigarette logos from both American and French cigarette packages. This first version of the subject was "a two-sided painting connected to a Tinguely sculpture that turned slowly allowing you to stand in one place as the other side of the work automatically came into view." [37] Shortly after its completion, Rivers and Tinguely showed the piece at the Musée des Arts Décoratifs of the Louvre. Some months later the Paris gallery Rive Droite featured many of Rivers' popular imagery works from the Tibor de Nagy exhibition of the previous year. His friendship with Tinguely and Niki de Saint-Phalle, Tinguely's companion, as well as with Yves Klein, put Rivers in the midst of the 1960s Parisian art world.

Rivers' sentimental connection to Tinguely and Saint-Phalle has lasted over the years. *The Continuing Interest in Abstract Art: Letters from Jean Tinguely and Niki de Saint-Phalle* (1981; Pl. 39) contains imagery and writings that commemorate

their earlier creative relationship. An exquisite pastel, entitled *Tinguely and Rivers in 1978* (1998; Pl. 57), represents a further testimony to Rivers' heartfelt link to his Swiss collaborator.

The *Vocabulary Lessons* series constitutes Rivers' most significant series produced during the year in Paris. Dutifully attending French classes at the Alliance Française, he found his source material there. He became intrigued by the words for ordinary body parts, especially those that rarely come up in language class, and he began to use his new wife, Clarice, as the model for paintings and drawings of nudes and individual parts of the female body that he carefully labeled anatomically. These works are at once a tribute to Clarice's voluptuousness and an examination of the concrete as well as the abstract function of words. He cleverly equates the necessity of the artist to deconstruct the whole in order to learn how to draw the individual elements with the needs of a foreigner who must deconstruct a language into individual words to learn how to speak it. The centrality of words in

which the anatomical labels extend out from the figure into the surrounding space.

Rivers' homage to David's *Napoleon in His Study* (1812), entitled *The Greatest Homosexual* (1964; Pl. 32), is perhaps his most infamous Gallic-inspired masterpiece. Inspired by seeing the David at Washington's National Gallery of Art, Rivers actually based his picture on a reproduction he purchased at the time of his museum visit four years earlier. And in case not everyone got the reference to the French neoclassical master, Rivers stenciled David's name onto the lower left area of the painting. In a letter to Abram Lerner, then curator of Joseph H. Hirshhorn's collection and later the first director of the Smithsonian's Hirshhorn Museum and Sculpture Garden, Rivers wrote about the creation of this painting:

The Greatest Homosexual *is a work in the tradition of a contemporary artist "paying homage" to some brilliant ancestor. While I didn't "get up" at the National Gallery as did Matisse when he copied at the Louvre (I just bought a large color repro),* The Greatest Homosexual *nevertheless was guided by what happens in* Napoleon in His Study, *David's (if I may) MASTERPIECE. After many days of drawing, brushing, cutting, gluing, stenciling etc. on canvas, which necessitated repeated and detailed observations of the repro I couldn't avoid some obvious nontechnical conclusions. Given a right hand resting in the split of the cream vest, a gesture which by itself has come to represent Napoleon, the plump torso settled comfortably on the left hip, the careful curls and coif, the cliché of pursed lips and what self satisfaction I read into the rest of the face, I decided Napoleon was Gay. Now if he* wasn't *histories* [sic] Greatest Homosexual, *who was — Michelangelo?* [38]

these pictures demonstrates Rivers' prescient use of written language and pictures in a mode that anticipates the postmodernist use of words in the work of such younger artists as Jenny Holzer, Barbara Kruger, and Ken Aptekar.

Rivers expanded the French *Vocabulary Lessons* series to include versions in English, Italian, and Polish, but the French ones clearly are the paradigm. *Parts of the Face: French Vocabulary Lesson* (1961; Pl. 23) shows Clarice's face, rendered in elegant detail though with only a single eye, dissected by radiating lines that attach to stenciled French words for every component of the human visage. The labels are set off by brushy blocks of color applied in broad abstract expressionist gestures. The face is not so much depicted as documented. Rivers extended the series to sculptures as well. He used department store mannequins to cast three-dimensional versions of the nudes, from

The irony and humor, as well as the innovative treatment of the painting surface, represent quintessential aspects of Rivers' approach to his subjects then and afterward. Like his earlier full-length figures in *Washington Crossing the Delaware* and *Self-Figure,* there is one fully realized figure and other, sketchier ghosts of the same image in partial form. Rivers eliminates almost all of the setting in David's composition but does include the clock above Napoleon's left shoulder and some lyrical decorative details lifted from the neoclassical relief on the wall to the left, reminiscent of embellishments found in *Boy in Blue Denim* (1955; Pl. 9).

Rivers was living in London, enjoying a residency at the Slade School of Fine Arts, when he painted Napoleon and developed the use of collage elements – like wooden cutouts or stencils – that exaggerate certain areas of the composition, creating an unexpected three-dimensional effect. Such an approach deliberately subverts the goal of old master painting, which was to create the visual perception of depth by modeling forms and situating them in a perspectival composition. His use of the attached pieces also works differently from the classic use of collage as employed by Picasso and Braque. They pasted fragments onto the surface of the composition to emphasize a sense of its fundamental flatness. Rivers' fragments make three-dimensionality literal, achieving a different kind of spatial interplay between the raised and planar surfaces. In the 1980s and 1990s Rivers built on this concept of enlivening the painted surface by making it partially three-dimensional with his use of carvable foamcore, as in *The Auction* (Pl. 54). Despite his differences and departures from the work of the earlier artists, Rivers' frame of reference in *The Greatest Homosexual* clearly derives from the French old master tradition, in his elegant drawing, formal conceits, and preference for a grandiose subject.

Rivers' tongue-in-cheek, off-the-wall kind of humor does not appeal to everyone. *The Greatest Homosexual,* now in the Hirshhorn Museum's collection, was at first rejected by Joseph Hirshhorn; he had decided not to buy it unless Rivers changed the title. Rivers refused and, in the end, Hirshhorn bought it anyway. In his autobiography Rivers tells the story of a Frenchman outraged by the painting on seeing it at the Hirshhorn Museum. "In a letter to the museum [he] requested its removal, asking how we Americans would feel coming across a painting of George Washington, the father of *our* country, called, in effect, *The Greatest Cocksucker.*" [39]

I Like Olympia in Blackface (1970; Pl. 36), probably rivals *The Greatest Homosexual* in raising the hackles of those uninitiated into Rivers' world. Taking off from Edouard Manet's *Olympia* (1863), Rivers chose to treat the image as a kind of relief – what could be called a shaped canvas – offering two versions of the scene. On top is a campy version of the original picture, showing a black maid displaying a recently arrived bouquet to her mistress, an odalisque brazenly looking out at the viewer while clad only in a necklace, a bracelet, and a pair of dainty, backless bedroom slippers. On the bottom, superimposed on the lower part of the upper scene, is the same subject with the race of the figures reversed: Olympia is now black and the maid is white.

The mixed response to Rivers' *Olympia* matched the largely negative reaction to Manet's painting when it was shown at the Paris Salon in 1865. Critic and poet Théophile Gautier announced that it could "be understood from no point of view, even if you take it for what it is, a puny model

Rivers playing the saxophone
with Steve Smith at the Bluebird,
Riverhead, Long Island
(Hans Namuth)

stretched out on a sheet. . . . Here is nothing, we are sorry to say, but the desire to attract attention at any price."[40] These sentiments could surely be shared by many viewing Rivers' version for the first time. As with David's *Napoleon,* Rivers chose to create a link between himself and a venerated French predecessor.

In 1970, when Rivers created *Olympia,* political discussions about race, along with those about the Vietnam War, still defined American society. The first half of 1970 was filled with turmoil: the continuation of the tumultuous trial of the Chicago Seven resulting from demonstrations at the 1968 Democratic Convention; protests against the Vietnam War, including the firebombing of buildings at the University of Wisconsin; the shooting of students at Kent State University; and the destruction of a town house in Greenwich Village where the Weathermen had been making bombs.[41] In addition, New Haven and Yale University were the site of a May Day rally in support of nine Black Panthers on trial for murder, and, in September, clashes between demonstrators and police erupted during the Revolutionary People's Constitutional Convention in Philadelphia sponsored by the Black Panthers and other black groups.[42]

Rivers was no newcomer to the world of race relations. Beginning in his teen years, when he had begun to play with jazz ensembles often dominated by African American musicians, he developed a deep sense of the problematic plight of blacks in America, at the same time as he understood them to be at the center of his musical universe. He struggled with the arbitrariness of their disadvantaged status in earlier works such as *Identification Manual* (1964), where he challenges sophistic notions of beauty based on racial background and their ludicrous role in America's preoccupation with race. In the same work, he includes auxiliary scenes based on press photographs at the height of the civil rights movement. And when Jasper Johns did his map of America in the early 1960s, Rivers did his *Africa II* (1962–63), a map of the "black continent." As one black writer put it, "In tackling . . . black life and history, Larry Rivers brings . . . his unique proximity to the black community, and his tendency to draw on this 'intimacy' to make art of his own life."[43] Without exaggerating, one can say that when dealing with black subjects, Rivers is able to draw upon genuine experiences that give unexpected legitimacy to the results.

ART AND ARTISTS. David and Manet represent only two of the many artists from the history of art Rivers has chosen to engage during his long career. From Bonnard, Courbet, Leutze, Géricault, and de Kooning in the 1940s and 1950s, to Barnett Newman, Rembrandt, Matisse, Picasso, and Miró in later years, much of Rivers' art has been an homage to and a commentary on the art of others. In 1993 he exhibited a series of works in New York at the Marlborough Gallery entitled *Art and the Artist.* This group of works represented Rivers' most extensive treatment of some of his favorite "old

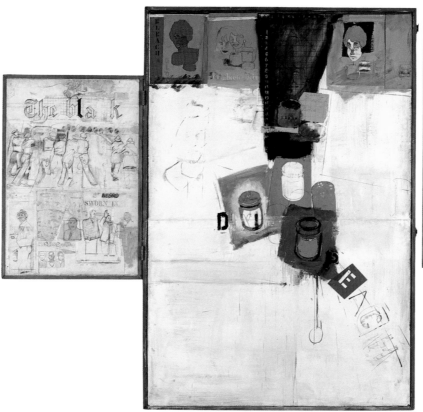

Identification Manual, 1964
Mixed media and collage on
fiberboard
73⅝ x 84⅜ x 19 in.
Smithsonian American Art
Museum, Washington, D.C.
Gift of Container Corporation
of America

masters" of the twentieth century, showing, as one critic put it, "his genuine love for the paintings he pirates."[44] Rivers says the series pays homage to "paintings that have been a part of my life."[45]

For each example, Rivers selected a characteristic work, or composite, and painted a version of it with the artist's own portrait included in the composition. *Art and the Artist: Picasso and the Bull* (1992; Pl. 51) features an image based on Picasso's *Bullfight* (1934). In another version, *The Bull, Algerian Women, and Picasso* (1992), Rivers combines references from two Picasso paintings: the same *Bullfight* and *Women of Algiers After Delacroix* (1955). Given the fact that *Bullfight* provides elements for Picasso's *Guernica* (1937), which in turn draws upon Guido Reni's *Massacre of the Innocents* (1611), while *Women of Algiers* derives from Delacroix's *Women of Algiers* (1834), Rivers has managed to create an art-historical palimpsest.

Rivers executed his *Art and the Artist* series in oil on canvas mounted on foamcore, giving the images his signature three-dimensionality, a kind of relief treatment that adds to the visual immediacy of the picture while it also communicates clearly Rivers' appropriation and reshaping of material that originated elsewhere. Different parts jump out at you at different angles, creating a slightly disorienting experience. Rivers' composite *Picasso* makes for an oddly coherent composition, with its playful take on the master contrasting effectively with the uncanny likeness of the artist handily inserted in front of the bull, next to the horse. Picasso on occasion used a bull as a stand-in for himself. Perhaps we have here a double portrait of the artist, a chameleon capable of taking many shapes in his creative pursuit. In keeping with Rivers' penchant for irony, could he also be, as a reviewer suggests, "making fun of the middle-brow cult of the celebrity genius," while also expressing admiration?[46]

Rivers' treatment of Matisse's *Harmony in Red* (1908), which he entitles *Déjà Vu and the Red Room: Double Portrait of Matisse* (1996; Pl. 56), functions much the same way. He has chosen a magnificently decorative scene – the elegant blue wall design against a red background extends without a break onto the tablecloth – where the maid can be interpreted as an alter ego for the artist. This is not a table set for eating, but rather, as Pierre Schneider observed, "a feast for the eyes . . . that the servant is occupied with arranging a still life," and that the servant's activity can be seen "as a metaphor for that of the artist."[47] Presumably the "double portrait" refers to both the actual likeness of Matisse in the upper right corner and the maid in her role as surrogate artist.

Rivers has done similar treatments of other favorite artists, including *Personage on the Lam* (1990; Pl. 47), *Léger at the Easel: Apache Cap* (1991; Pl. 50), and *Art and the Artist: Miró* (1993-95; Pl. 52). The first, a salute to Wilfredo Lam, is as witty as it is astute. The composition, extrapolated from Lam's signature surrealist-abstract style, evokes the spirit of the artist while also taking a good-natured potshot at Lam's humorless mindset. Rivers' take on Léger is equally clever, achieving a likeness of the artist that resembles his work. Rivers used Léger's *Homage to Louis David* (1948-49) as the basis for his composition.[48] According to Rivers, the "Apache Cap" refers to the kind of hat worn by the male in performances of a popular Parisian dance (the apache) featured in old movies.[49] In discussing his Léger painting, Rivers said he had gotten his inspiration from seeing a photo of Léger working in his studio: "You couldn't tell where he ended and the work began. . . . I want to show the artist in the work, as part of it."[50] Miró, another of Rivers' idols, looks at once playful and studious in his portrait set against a Miróesque fragment composed of his characteristic colors and shapes. In an interview during the period Rivers was working on the Miró, he confessed that he felt somewhat bereft of living

artist role models. "I don't have any heroes anymore – all my heroes are dead."[51]

Although not connected to France, as were so many of Rivers' dead heroes, Rembrandt van Rijn certainly enjoys a major presence in Rivers' repertoire, beginning in the early 1960s with his first *Dutch Masters* painting. Rivers describes the genesis of the series this way:

One night . . . on the Long Island Expressway entering the Midtown Tunnel, I saw a neon billboard version of Rembrandt's Syndics of the Drapery [*or* Clothmakers'] Guild, *supposedly representing the craftsmanship that went into the making of Dutch Masters Cigars. That billboard, combined with my recent experience painting a lot of American and French cigarette packs, stoked the fires ad infinitum for my "Dutch Masters" series, which comprises everything from an eight-by-ten-inch color pencil drawing to a ten-foot 3-D version.*[52]

As he had done with David's *Napoleon,* Rivers chose to work from an image at least one step removed from the original old master picture. Rivers has often pointed out that he can paint from memory but prefers the ease of working from an already existing subject he finds easily accessible. "I can draw from imagination, but I prefer to look at visual information based on someone else's effort, like reproductions and photos."[53] In *Dutch Masters I* (1963; Pl. 30) Rivers takes a painterly approach to his rendering of the familiar cigar box image, treating the words on the product package as cavalierly as the figures from Rembrandt's original group portrait. Although executed during a trying period in Rembrandt's career – after the death of his companion Hendrickje, when he was alone and financially at risk – this picture commis-

Packing the Dutch Masters, 1997
Oil on canvas mounted on
sculpted foamcore
97 x 63 x 7½ in.
The Corcoran Gallery of Art,
Washington, D.C.
Gift of Mr. and Mrs. Jeffrey Loria in
memory of Harriet Loria Popowitz

explanation for such an arbitrary choice of subject, Rivers commented, "We're so programmed to that idea that you have to go onward and upward to something new and something advanced. It's really getting boring, as you want to do something old." [54]

In a second version of the scene, *Dutch Masters and Cigars II* (1963; Pl. 31), Rivers delineates the features of the six figures in more detail, with applications of collaged elements. He also matches the picture with the reason for its contemporary prominence on the billboards of America: the cigars – lying in their box, looking as much like frankfurters as cigars. The sexual gag is difficult to ignore and becomes even more pronounced in some of the later versions he produced from time to time over the succeeding decades. This is particularly true of *Packing the Dutch Masters* (1997), Rivers' foamcore rendition of the cigar box with cigars.

Besides Rivers' salutes to artists of the past, he has often done portraits of his artist friends. *De Kooning with My Texas Hat* (1963; Pl. 29), a drawing, shows Rivers' talent as a draftsman appropriately reminiscent of de Kooning in his early figurative work. Rivers felt especially warm toward de Kooning, who early on expressed his appreciation for Rivers' talent. In an often-cited quote, de Kooning said Rivers' painting was like "pressing your face into wet grass." [55] According to notes in the Hirshhorn's archives, Rivers

sioned by the Clothmakers' Guild was rivaled, according to scholars, only by Frans Hals' *Regents of the Old Men's Almshouse* and *Regentesses of the Old Men's Almshouse* (both 1664). The direct manner in which the sitters engage the viewer, still visible in the schlocky Dutch Masters cigar box reproduction, must have appealed to Rivers; even at such a drastic remove from the source, they caught his attention as he casually passed them by. In one

made the portrait . . . during a visit with de Kooning in Springs (a community in the Hamptons on Long Island). De Kooning was telling a story about a woman and Rivers found the story boring, so he decided to do a drawing while he listened to Bill finish the story. He also mentioned that he had such admiration for de Kooning as a draftsman. Not many people realize that, although de Kooning is known for his gestural style, his early drawings were like "Old Master" drawing – although they also looked modern.[56]

With characteristic cynicism, Rivers produced at least three versions of this portrait by making tracings from the original.[57]

Rivers took an entirely different approach in another artist portrait – his *Jim Dine Storm Window* (1965; Pl. 34), done during a period in which he experimented with many new materials such as Plexiglas, electric lighting, and plastics. Using a wood panel as the primary support, attached to the back of a storm window fixture, Rivers enhanced his painted image by applying three-dimensional collaged pieces that give the portrait an elemental, visceral quality. Rivers has said "this is the only work I ever dreamed." He recalled that he "was returning from Europe on a boat . . . fell asleep in the middle of the afternoon . . . and . . . dreamed of Jim Dine in a storm window."[58]

Very early in his career, Rivers had created cutout portraits,[59] attached to the outside of their frames, that may be related to the Dine executed more than a decade later. Despite its pronounced material presence, the Dine portrait also has an otherworldly aspect to it, as if Dine has become inexplicably one with the window through which we see him. According to Rivers, "the pleasure of this window is that it opens and shuts, and you can get three views."[60] Rivers used this technique for his portrait of Trotsky in *The History of the Russian Revolution* (1965) and for a portrait of Jean Tinguely (1965).

Almost a decade later, Rivers captured abstract artist Barnett Newman in a painting, *The Stripe Is in the Eye of the Beholder*, and in a large-scale drawing of the same composition and name (1975;

Pl. 37). For Rivers, Newman is the quintessential abstract artist, categorical and unyielding in his conviction of nonobjectivity's superiority and rectitude. Based on a photograph taken by Paul Katz, the works show Newman seated before *Sixth Station* (1962), a canvas from his series *Stations of the Cross.* Newman had first exhibited this series at New York's Guggenheim Museum in 1966 (April–June), a couple of months after Rivers' retrospective at the Jewish Museum. Its thrust – a Jewish take on Christ not as the Messiah, but as a representative of human suffering – likely impressed Rivers. Newman's triumphant retrospective at the Museum of Modern Art, with an accompanying catalog by Rivers' close friend Tom Hess, took place in 1971, four years before the painting and drawing.

Newman's portrait shows Rivers in a very different mode from the painterly treatment of such subjects as the early *Dutch Masters* pieces. Here Rivers achieves an almost photorealist likeness, sticking with the black and white of the photograph, the same two-color palette Newman maintained throughout the fourteen canvases of his series. While the painting has an airbrushed quality, the drawing is gritty and exacting, with smudges and tiny details only enhancing the remarkable likeness. Humor, however, survives. Rivers has added an extra translucent stripe passing right through Newman's right eye, to which the title refers, and Rivers playfully signs his name just under the bottom right edge of Newman's canvas where Newman has signed *his* name. The canvas has such a material presence in the picture that the effect comes close to trompe l'oeil.

Rivers executed his 1986 portrait of the Lichtensteins, Roy and his wife Dorothy, in oil on canvas mounted on foamcore, a technique he perfected in the mid-1980s. Entitled *Cubism Today: Broad*

Merce Cunningham: Seated, 1996
Oil on canvas
60 x 43 in.
Marlborough Gallery, New York

Stroke (Pl. 41), it depicts the two inserted amidst a field of jagged geometric forms in variable depths, as if they had been caught in a whimsical trap of cubist debris. Several variations on the Lichtensteins exist, all punning on art history as Lichtenstein so often did in his late work that referenced modern old masters. The Lichtenstein pictures suggest a kinship between Rivers' anthology of artistic mentors and their works and Lichtenstein's reexamination and re-presentation of iconic images such as Monet's cathedrals and Van Gogh's bed-

room, demonstrating a similar ability to capture a certain essence tempered by a tongue-in-cheek irreverence.

SHOWBIZ. Rivers, if not born a showman, grew into such a talent early in life. From his childhood performances as his father's accompanist, to his career as a jazz musician and, more recently, the exhibitionistic narrative that constitutes his 1992 autobiography, he has made it clear that he knows how to capture an audience. Rivers even participated actively as a performer in off-Broadway theater and experimental movies during the 1950s and 1960s, and again in the 1980s. Moreover, a sometimes crude, self-deprecating sense of humor has contributed to the theatrics that have often put Rivers in the spotlight. Some have mistakenly interpreted his tendency not to take art and the art world entirely on its own, sometimes pretentious terms as a lack of seriousness. With Rivers as with so much of life, humor can be the soul of truth. Rivers' lighthearted take on his own life, along with the objective details – a ménage with mother-in-law as muse; spectacular success on a famous quiz show; near death at the hands of African guerrilla fighters; jazz and drugs; parades of girlfriends as well as a few boyfriends; dramatic ups and downs in the world of high art sweepstakes – could be dream material for a documentary screenwriter.

Rivers' colorful life appears to have given him a taste for subjects from the entertainment world that appear prominently in his art. He has often depicted his performer friends, including musicians like Sonny Simmons and dancers such as Merce Cunningham, as well as icons drawn from the movies – Fred Astaire and Greta Garbo, for example. He has also created works related to the experience of moviegoing in such mixed-media

Miss Popcorn, 1972
Acrylic on canvas
72 x 43 in.
Museo del Arte Contemporaneo,
Caracas, Venezuela

pieces from the 1970s as *Miss Popcorn* (1972), and *Movie House* (1972). In the late 1990s, Rivers did a series of four mural-scale canvases presenting a kaleidoscopic history of American movies. The period he covers, the golden age of the American cinema, before independent movies and little-known actors, parallels the sweep of Rivers' career from his beginnings as the James Dean of the art world to his current old master status as an exalted Marlon Brando figure – everyone remembers when he was determined to defy conventional norms, yet his bravura talent is what continues to loom large even today.

A jazzman since his teens, Rivers has maintained a strong connection to the world of musicians, especially fellow saxophone players, clubs, and performers of all kinds. Two of his pictures devoted to the black saxophonist Sonny Simmons capture both his admiration and his preoccupation

Movie House, 1972
Mixed-media construction
72 ¼ x 184 ¾ x 6 in.
Marlborough Gallery, New York

with the peculiarities of the jazz world. And while Rivers' model for these pictures is Sonny Simmons, Rivers greatly admired still another saxophone-playing Sonny – Sonny Rollins. In both *Umber Blues II, Sonny on the Side Relief* (1987; Pl. 42), and *Umber Blues: Sonny and Picasso's "Three Musicians"* (1993; Pl. 53), Rivers links blackness with performance both on the stage and in the bedroom. In the latter, he also draws a parallel between the sexual prowess and the artistry of the black musician and those same attributes as embodied by Picasso, renowned not only for his artistic talent but for his sexual magnetism even in old age. Instead of a portrait of the artist himself, as in the Picasso takeoffs from the *Art and the Artist* series, Rivers substitutes Picasso's *Three Musicians* (1921) to represent the artist. Amusingly, Sonny is seated directly in front of Picasso's horn player, adorned appropriately with a black mask.

Rivers likes dancers as well. Fred Astaire appears in many paintings beginning in the mid-1980s, reflecting Rivers' eclectic interest in both the movies and the science of movement. Although Astaire had already appeared in one of Rivers' diaristic panoramas, *Public and Private* (1984-85), his interest in the dancer's physical feats increased after his encounter with the early work of English vorticist David Bomberg.[61] The vorticists, like the Italian futurists, focused on scientific experiments dealing with speed and motion that they expressed in their own cubist-inspired style. *Dancing with Bomberg's Dancer* (1990; Pl. 48), with its angular forms exaggerated by Rivers' carved foamcore surface, reflects his appreciation for Bomberg as well as Astaire, and for the way different cultures – in this case science and the performing arts – intersect in the modern world, cross-fertilizing each other.[62]

Rivers' dual focus on science/technology and the performing arts surfaces again in his paintings featuring Charlie Chaplin from the 1936 movie *Modern Times,* Chaplin's last silent film, for which he is remembered as the director, the principal actor, as well as the composer. A comic diatribe (albeit silent) against the evils of technology, the movie has many memorable scenes. Rivers chooses one of the most famous, Chaplin lying on top of a giant gear in the midst of a complex network of other gears and industrial machinery (Pl. 45). The gears bear an uncanny resemblance to old-fashioned movie reels, and the style suggests that Léger's construction or acrobat pictures may have served as an inspiration.[63]

Rivers returned to the subject of silent films in his series *A Vanished World.* Two works picturing Greta Garbo and John Gilbert from the 1927 MGM blockbuster *Flesh and the Devil* recreate famous still photos from this celebrated movie. Garbo and Gilbert starred in three silent films together, but critics tout *Flesh and the Devil* as their best collaboration. The caption for *Garbo and Gilbert I* (1994; Pl. 55) in the collection of *The Silents Majority,* an online journal, reads: "Drunk on Love. The most famous clinch of the silent era."[64] The story revolves around a romantic triangle, with Garbo as the irresistible femme fatale who inserts herself between two close friends. In this scene, Garbo's expressive face shows her succumbing to Gilbert's passionate embrace. The juxtaposition of Garbo, considered one of the most beautiful actresses in the history of the cinema, with that of "the most charismatic of all her leading men,"[65] still makes for an arresting image. Rivers enhances the intimacy and the immediacy of the lovers with his three-dimensional foamcore treatment. He also exaggerates the diagonals and intricate relationship of the geometric

History of Hollywood:
Part I, 1999
Oil on canvas
82 x 110 in.
Private Collection, New York

elements of the image. The narrative component and the formal organization reinforce each other with Rivers' characteristic finesse. The sensitive use of color and decorative embellishment of the clothing and fabrics also contributes to its visual effectiveness. *Garbo and Gilbert II* (1994) pictures another embrace given the same Rivers treatment. The *Silents Majority* caption is equally romantic: "She lured him out of the cold and into a cozy room with fires blazing . . ." Even several times removed from its origin, in Rivers' hands, the visual result is powerful and irresistible.

In 1999, Rivers began an epic series called *History of Hollywood.* So far he has completed four major canvases and may do others. These works, done in oil on canvas, show that Rivers remains comfortable with a traditional approach to painting despite his emphasis in recent years on the foamcore pieces. The series offers not only an amalgam of recognizable images and scenes from major productions, it also contains elements that have particular resonance for

Rivers personally. Betty Boop, a favorite cartoon personality from the past, appears prominently. Rivers has had a larger than life-size statue of this character in his home for years as a kind of mascot. The choice of King Kong, too, may relate to his fascination with the animals – particularly the ones from Africa – in the Bronx Zoo, located just across the street from the building where he grew up. Moreover, as a sometime movie actor himself, he feels a connection to those who appear on the silver screen. And, similar to his interest in the major creators who played key roles in the history of art, Rivers appreciates the influential movie directors who have deeply affected filmmaking. Alfred Hitchcock is shown here in connection with his unforgettable 1963 film, *The Birds.*

A similar panoramic presentation characterizes *History of Hollywood: Part IV* (2000; Pl. 58). Many old favorites from earlier in the series make another appearance: Marlon Brando, Audrey Hepburn, Groucho Marx, Elizabeth Taylor, and Judy Garland.

History of Hollywood:
Part II, 1999
Oil on canvas
77½ x 104½ in.
Private Collection, New York

History of Hollywood:
Part III, 2000
Oil on canvas
76½ x 112 in.
Private Collection, New York

Rivers with *History of Hollywood*
series, Southampton, 2000
(David C. Levy)

Rivers with his Betty Boop
sculpture, Southampton, 1999
(David C. Levy)

But instead of Dorothy with her sidekicks, we have
a close-up of the *Wizard of Oz* heroine closely
linked to her ruby shoes. Elizabeth Taylor appears
not only in *Raintree County,* as before, but in her
role as Cleopatra. Other figures relate to this Hollywood series as well as to Rivers' longer-term
engagement with movie icons such as Charlie Chaplin and Fred Astaire. Rivers readily admits that such
recycling is central to his approach. "I use everything three or four times," he said recently. "You

don't have to do as much work. You have the source
materials right there."[66] With or without repeti-
tions, Rivers weaves disparate images drawn from
movie stills and advertisements into a masterful
exegesis of this rich area of American culture. His
selection of quintessential examples inspires personal associations across several generations, providing the most current example of Rivers' capacity
to grasp and communicate not only his experience
of the world but our own.

NOTES

1. Frank O'Hara, *Art Chronicles 1954–1966* (New York: Braziller, 1975), p. 118.
2. Martin Tschechne, "The Last Hippie," trans. Elizabeth Cats, *Art* (German) (October 1992): typescript, p. 10.
3. The exhibition catalog was published as *Larry Rivers: Public and Private* (Youngstown, Ohio: Butler Institute of American Art, 1990).
4. Fiamma Arditi, "Larry Rivers," trans. from Italian by Peter Glendenning (1994): typescript, p. 3. In Rivers' Studio Archive.
5. Ibid.
6. Larry Rivers with Carol Brightman, *Drawings and Digressions* (New York: Clarkson N. Potter, 1979), p. 45.
7. Larry Rivers with Arnold Weinstein, *What Did I Do? The Unauthorized Autobiography* (New York: Harper Collins, 1992), p. 65 (hereafter, *Autobiography*).
8. Robert Enright, "The Juice and the Joy of It: The Art and Life of Larry Rivers," *Border Crossings* 13, no. 3 (summer 1994): 48.
9. Leo Steinberg, "Month in Review: Contemporary Group of New York Painters at Stable Gallery," *Arts Magazine* 30 (January 1956): 48.
10. O'Hara, *Art Chronicles,* p. 114.
11. Ibid.
12. David Lehman, "O'Hara's Artful Life," *Art in America* 88, no. 2 (February 2000): 119.
13. See Germain Bazin, *Théodore Géricault: Etude critique, documents et catalogue raisonée,* vol. 2 (Paris: Fondation Wildenstein, 1987).
14. See *Proof Positive: Forty Years of Contemporary American Printmaking, 1957–1997* (Washington, D.C.: Corcoran Gallery of Art, 1997), particularly Plate 1, *Stones: Five O'Clock* (1958).
15. *When the Sun Tries to Go On* (1970) and *The Art of Love* (1974). See, for example, Rivers with Brightman, *Drawings and Digressions,* pp. 124-26 and 128-29.
16. Marlborough Fine Arts was founded in London in 1946 and opened its first New York gallery in 1963 under the name Marlborough-Gerson.
17. Sam Hunter, "Larry Rivers," in *Rivers* (New York: Abrams/Meridian Modern Artists, 1971), p. 33.
18. Peter Schjeldahl, "Larry Rivers: Achingly Erratic," *New York Times,* December 27, 1970.
19. The painting was partially destroyed in a fire at the Museum of Modern Art in 1958. It was restored. Another painting with the same title, painted in 1960, is in the collection of the Whitney Museum of American Art.
20. Harold Rosenberg, "The American Action Painters," *ARTnews* 51 (December 1952): 22.
21. *Autobiography,* p. 310.
22. Ibid.
23. O'Hara, *Art Chronicles,* p. 111.
24. Larry Rivers, "A Discussion of the Work of Larry Rivers," *ARTnews* 60, no. 1 (March 1961): 54.
25. Emily Genauer, "'Sensational' Show at the Jewish Museum," *New York Herald Tribune,* September 29, 1965.
26. Emily Genauer, "Revolution by Rivers," *New York Herald Tribune*, October 3, 1965.
27. See complete text in Avrahn Yarmolinsky, ed., *An Anthology of Russian Verse, 1812–1960* (Garden City, N.Y.: Doubleday, 1962), p. 153.
28. William Berkson, "The Sculpture of Larry Rivers," *Arts Magazine* 40, no. 1 (November 1965): 52.
29. Enright, "The Juice and the Joy," 49.
30. Furio Colombo, "Larry Rivers," in Achille Bonito Oliva and Furio Colombo, *Larry Rivers: One Man Show* (Rome: Galleria d'Arte il Gabbiano, 1992), p. 18.
31. Peter Hellman and Beate Karlsfeld, *The Auschwitz Album: A Book Based Upon an Album Discovered by a Concentration Camp Survivor, Lili Neider* (New York: Random House, 1981).
32. Sam Hunter, "Larry Rivers: Public and Private," in *Larry Rivers: Public and Private,* p. 8.

33. Peter Kolchin, *American Slavery, 1619–1877* (New York: Hill & Wang, 1994). I have not been able to determine the original source of this image, but Rivers used it earlier in his series *Some American History*. See *Some American History* (Houston: Institute for the Arts, Rice University, 1971), fig. 3.

34. Ruth Bass, "Larry Rivers: Marlborough," *ARTnews* 93, no. 8 (October 1994): 180.

35. *Autobiography,* p. 390.

36. Barbaralee Diamonstein, "Larry Rivers," interview with Larry Rivers in *Inside New York's Art World* (New York: Rizzoli, 1979), p. 328.

37. *Autobiography,* p. 39.

38. Abram Lerner, ed., *The Hirshhorn Museum and Sculpture Garden* (New York: Harry Abrams, 1974), p. 739, quoted in Phyllis Rosenzweig, ed., *Larry Rivers: The Hirshhorn Museum and Sculpture Garden Collection* (Washington, D.C.: Smithsonian Institution Press, 1981), p. 41.

39. *Autobiography,* p. 375.

40. John Rewald, *The History of Impressionism* (New York: Museum of Modern Art, 1973), pp. 123–124.

41. Nancy Zaroulis and Gerald Sullivan, *Who Spoke Up? American Protest Against the War in Vietnam 1963–1975* (Garden City, N.Y.: Doubleday, 1984), pp. 301–320.

42. Norma Sayre, *Sixties Going on Seventies* (New Brunswick, N.J.: Rutgers University Press, 1996), pp. 46–52; 116–123.

43. Charles Childs, "Larry Ocean Swims the Nile, Mississippi and Other Rivers," in *Some American History,* p. 12.

44. Ruth Bass, "Larry Rivers: Marlborough," *ARTnews* 92, no. 6 (summer 1993): 168.

45. Helen A. Harrison, "Larry Rivers Fills In Some of the Blanks," *New York Times,* Long Island edition, August 23, 1992.

46. Ken Johnson, "Larry Rivers at Marlborough," *Art in America* 81, no. 5 (May 1993): 117.

47. Pierre Schneider, *Matisse* (New York: Rizzoli, 1984), p. 316.

48. *Fernand Léger: Five Themes and Variations* (New York: Solomon R. Guggenheim Museum, 1962), p. 49.

49. Interview with the author, September 28, 2001.

50. Harrison, "Larry Rivers Fills In. . . ."

51. Barbara A. MacAdam, "Still Raging Rivers: 'Cool,' Contrarian, and Gregarious, Larry Rivers Continues to Provoke," *ARTnews* 93, no. 3 (November 1994): 150.

52. *Autobiography,* p. 355.

53. Ibid., p. 310.

54. Jeffrey H. Loria, "Golden Oldies: An Interview with Larry Rivers," *Arts Magazine* 53, no. 3 (November 1978): 106.

55. Sam Hunter, *Larry Rivers* (New York: Arthur Bartley, 1989), p. 50.

56. Notes by Judith Zilczer on Rivers' visit April 20, 1993, Archives of the Hirshhorn Museum and Sculpture Garden, Smithsonian Institution.

57. One version is in the collection of the Arkansas Art Center, and art critic John Russell purchased another when he and Rivers met in London during Rivers' residency at the Slade School of Fine Arts.

58. Rivers and Brightman, *Drawings and Digressions,* p. 199.

59. Helen A. Harrison, *Larry Rivers* (New York: ARTnews Books, 1984), pp. 32–33.

60. Rivers and Brightman, *Drawings and Digressions,* p. 199.

61. Hunter, *Larry Rivers,* p. 41.

62. For a discussion of Rivers' use of foamcore, see Ruth Bass, "Larry Rivers' Canvas Cut-Ups," *ARTnews* 85, no. 8 (October 1986): 86–90.

63. See *Acrobat and Jugglers* (1953) in *Fernand Léger: Five Themes and Variations,* p. 87.

64. Diane MacIntyre, *The Silents Majority,* 1996–97, at *www.silentsmajority.com.*

65. Ibid.

66. Interview with the author, September 28, 2001.

Overleaf: **Plate 40,** *The Continuing Interest in Abstract Art: From Photos of Gwynne and Emma Rivers* (detail)

PLATES

PLATE 1. **Berdie** 1952, bronze

PLATE 2. Self-Figure 1953, oil on canvas

PLATE 3. **Washington Crossing the Delaware**

1953, oil, graphite, and charcoal on linen

PLATE 4. Berdie Seated 1953, bronze sculpture

PLATE 5. Berdie Seated I 1953, painted plaster sculpture

PLATE 6. O'Hara Nude with Boots

1954, oil on canvas

PLATE 7. Portrait of a Man (John Bernard Myers) 1954, oil on canvas

PLATE 8. The Family 1954–55, oil on canvas

PLATE 9. Boy in Blue Denim (Portrait of Steven) 1955, oil on canvas

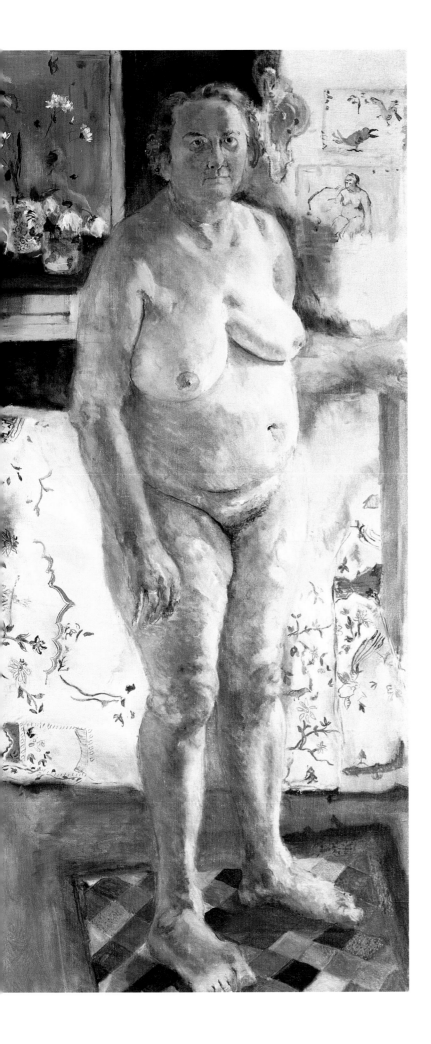

PLATE 10. Double Portrait of Berdie 1955, oil on canvas

PLATE 12. The 25 Cent Summer Cap   1956, oil and charcoal on canvas

PLATE 13. Berdie with the American Flag 1957, oil on canvas

PLATE 14. **Stones: Five O'Clock** 1958, lithograph (Larry Rivers and Frank O'Hara)

BERDIE

How lucky we are that you're
in so many museums
so we can go and look
and be out of traffic
as if we were talking
in the dirty light
of loss

it is not the Parthenon
but a Vuillard small
as an Adam's apple
where pain mounts and falls

IV

group of single copies put together 10/24/66
Rivers

PLATE 15. **Stones: Berdie**   1959, lithograph (Larry Rivers and Frank O'Hara)

PLATE 16. Me in a Rectangle   1959, oil on canvas

PLATE 17. Three Kings 1960, oil on canvas

PLATE 19. French Money

1961, oil on canvas

PLATE 20. Cedar Bar Menu II 1961, oil on canvas

PLATE 21. **Disque Bleu** 1961, oil on canvas

PLATE 22.
The Friendship of
America and France
(Kennedy and De Gaulle)
1961–62, repainted 1970,
oil on canvas

PLATE 23. Parts of the Face: French Vocabulary Lesson 1961, oil on canvas

PLATE 24. **How to Draw Series: Visage (Parts of the Face/Two Faces)** 1962, pencil, collage, and charcoal on paper

PLATE 25. How to Draw Series: Oreilles (Ears)   1962, gouache, pencil, charcoal, photomechanical reproductions, and cellophane tape on paper

PLATE 26. How to Draw: Eyes, Nose, and Mouth   1962, pencil, gouache, collage, and charcoal on paper

PLATE 27. Amel Camel 1962, oil on canvas on collage

PLATE 28. French Money ca. 1962, drawing

PLATE 29. De Kooning with My Texas Hat 1963, pencil, crayon, and cellophane tape on paper

PLATE 30. Dutch Masters I 1963, oil on canvas   **PLATE 31.** Dutch Masters and Cigars II 1963, oil and board collage on canvas

PLATE 33. **The History of the Russian Revolution from Marx to Mayakovsky**   1965, mixed media construction

1. Friedrich Engels (1820-95) and Karl Marx (1818-83) were the coauthors of the *Communist Manifesto,* 1848.

2. Prince Klemens von Metternich (1773-1859) was a statesman who restored Austria to great power status. As minister of foreign affairs, he established a system of international relations based on a common conservative platform. He advocated suppressing the liberal ideas and revolutionary movements that emerged in Europe during the first half of the nineteenth century. Metternich was forced to resign in March 1848.

3. "A-H Empire" refers to the Austro-Hungarian Empire, a multinational state that Metternich established during the Napoleonic era. Nationalist movements within the empire led eventually to the assassination of Archduke Francis Ferdinand, heir to the throne, at Sarajevo and to the outbreak of World War I in 1914. Sarajevo is the capital of contemporary Bosnia and Herzegovina.

4. "Louis B" refers to Louis Blanc (1811-82), the Frenchman who devised the socialist ideal "from each according to his ability, to each according to his need." Blanc was a utopian socialist and member of the provisional government in France after the February Revolution, the first in a series of reformist eruptions in Europe in 1848, all of which eventually failed.

5. The Commune of Paris controlled that city from March to May 1871. An experiment in municipal government, the Commune began as a coalition of radicals protesting the treaty ending the Franco-Prussian War (1870-71). The treaty had been negotiated by Adolphe Thiers (1797-1877), head of the French Assembly. Internal divisions within the Commune made it difficult to organize an effective defense, and the Communards were violently repressed by Thiers's government.

6. Prince Otto von Bismarck (1815-98), chancellor of the German Empire, negotiated the treaty with Thiers.

7. Czar Alexander II (1818-81) ruled Russia, the greatest land empire in Europe, from 1855 until 1881. In 1861, he abolished serfdom, but his reforms failed to satisfy peasants and radical intellectuals.

8. Based on nineteenth-century photographs, these images of Russian peasants evoke the plight of the rural underclass after their emancipation.

9. Nihilists, members of a reformist Russian party that encouraged assassination and terrorism, killed Alexander II in St. Petersburg on March 13, 1881.

10. Czar Nicholas II (1868-1918), Alexander II's successor, and Czarina Alexandra Feodorovna (d. 1918) appear dressed for a court ball at the Winter Palace in 1904.

11. The Duma, a legislative assembly, was established in 1905 by Nicholas II as a concession to popular demands. Nicholas II was forced to abdicate in March 1917, and a provisional revolutionary government took control of Russia.

12-14. These images relate to three revolutionary leaders – Leon Trotsky (1879-1940), Joseph Stalin (1879-1953), and Nikolai Lenin (1870-1924).

15. This map of Siberia includes Ekaterinburg, the site of the execution, by the Bolsheviks, of Nicholas II and his family on July 16, 1918. Also indicated are Volochanka and Verkhoyansk, sites of exile camps in the 1930s under Stalin's regime.

16. In the center of this map is a German military helmet that signifies World War I. Russia suffered heavy civilian casualties and territorial losses, including parts of Poland, during the war. The map includes Pskov, the city where Nicholas II abdicated in 1917, and Rapallo, Italy, the site where Germany and Russia signed an economic cooperation treaty in 1922.

17. Below this portrait of Lenin appear pages from his diary, including his warnings against Stalin: "He's not to be trusted."

18. Weapons of this type were used during World War I and the revolutionary period in Russia.

19. Violent mass demonstrations in Petrograd in July 1917 marked the Bolshevik party's premature attempt to seize power from the provisional revolutionary government and presaged the Russian Civil War (1918–20).

20. These images of Bolshevik (the Reds) and anti-Bolshevik (the Whites) troops are based on contemporary photographs.

21. Alexander Kerensky (1881–1970) served as prime minister of the provisional revolutionary government until its overthrow in October 1917 by the Reds. Irkutsk, a main stop on the Trans-Siberian Railway, was the site of the defeat of the Whites and the execution of their leader, Alexander Kolchak (1875–1920).

22. Stalin, "The Steel One," wrested power from Trotsky after Lenin's death in 1924.

23. Trotsky was accused of treason by Stalin and banished from the Soviet Union in 1929. After seeking refuge in several European countries, Trotsky fled to Mexico, where he was murdered in 1940.

24. On this tombstone appear the names of revolutionary martyrs, many of whom were killed or imprisoned by Stalin.

25. Maxim Gorky (1868–1936) was the author of many novels, including *Mother* (1907). Like Mayakovsky, Gorky originally supported the revolution. It is suspected that Stalin was instrumental in his death.

26. These images of mechanization symbolize the industrialization program inaugurated under Stalin's first Five-Year Plan (1928–32).

27. Under the scrawled "M" appear title pages, in several languages, of books by the revolutionary poet Vladimir Mayakovsky (1893–1930).

28. Pipes and coils, reminiscent of the found objects and constructions of such Dada artists as Marcel Duchamp (1887–1968), may also refer to Stalin's ruthless industrialization programs.

29. The "5s" refer to Stalin's ongoing Five-Year Plans.

30. The Russian word for "flying" is inscribed above a wood model of the Luger pistol that Mayakovsky used to commit suicide in 1930.

31. Mayakovsky appears with a gun pointed at his temple. To the far right is the text of his poem "The Worker Poet" (1918), which expressed his revolutionary fervor. The historical narrative ends with his tragic allusion to the idealistic spirit that gave birth to the revolution.

Courtesy of The Hirshhorn Museum and Sculpture Garden, Smithsonian Institution, Washington, D.C.

PLATE 34. **Jim Dine Storm Window** 1965, oil, pencil, and collage on aluminum and glass window and on screen mounted on plywood with wood frame

PLATE 35. Don't Fall 1966, electric construction

PLATE 36.

I Like Olympia in Blackface

1970, mixed media construction

PLATE 37. **The Stripe Is in the Eye of the Beholder (Portrait of Barnett Newman)**   1975, pencil and colored pencil on paper

PLATE 38. Golden Oldies of the 60s   1978, oil on canvas

PLATE 39. **The Continuing Interest in Abstract Art: Letters from Jean Tinguely and Niki de Saint-Phalle** 1981, mixed media on canvas

PLATE 40. **The Continuing Interest in Abstract Art: From Photos of Gwynne and Emma Rivers** 1981, mixed media on canvas

PLATE 41. Cubism Today: Broad Stroke   1986, oil on canvas mounted on sculpted foamcore

PLATE 42. Umber Blues II, Sonny on the Side Relief 1987, oil on canvas mounted on sculpted foamcore

PLATE 43. **Dancer in an Abstract Field: Fred Flying I**

1988, oil on canvas mounted on sculpted foamcore

PLATE 44. Primo Levi: Survivor 1987, oil on canvas mounted on sculpted foamcore

PLATE 45. **Modernist Times: Charlie Tightening the Bolts** 1989, oil on canvas mounted on sculpted foamcore

PLATE 46.

Four Seasons: Spring in the Forest of Birkenau

1990, oil on canvas mounted on sculpted foamcore

PLATE 47. Personage on the Lam 1990, oil on canvas mounted on sculpted foamcore

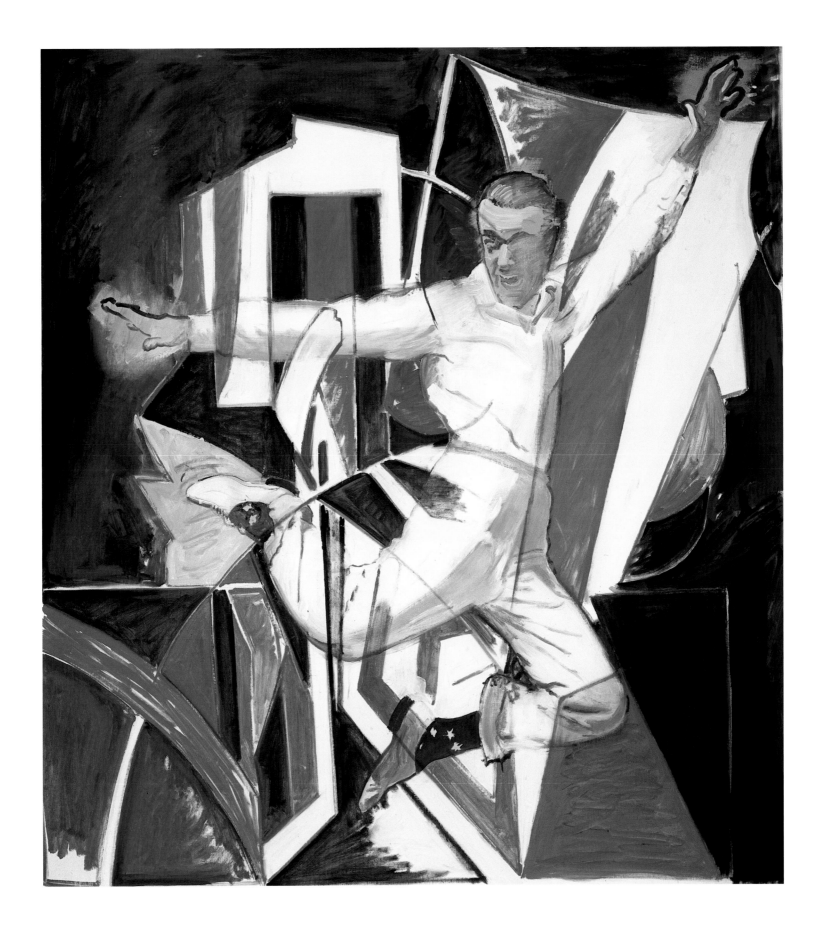

PLATE 48. **Dancing with Bomberg's Dancer**   1990, oil on canvas

PLATE 49. **Studio Interior** 1990–91, oil on canvas

PLATE 50. **Léger at the Easel: Apache Cap** 1991, oil on canvas mounted on sculpted foamcore

PLATE 51. Art and the Artist: Picasso and the Bull 1992, oil on canvas mounted on sculpted foamcore

PLATE 52. Art and the Artist: Miró 1993–95, oil on canvas mounted on sculpted foamcore

PLATE 53. Umber Blues: Sonny and Picasso's "Three Musicians"   1993, oil on canvas mounted on sculpted foamcore

PLATE 55. A Vanished World: Garbo and Gilbert I 1994, oil on canvas mounted on sculpted foamcore

PLATE 56. Déjà Vu and the Red Room: Double Portrait of Matisse (Harmony in Red) 1996, oil on canvas mounted on sculpted foamcore

PLATE 57. Tinguely and Rivers in 1978 1998, pastel and pencil on paper

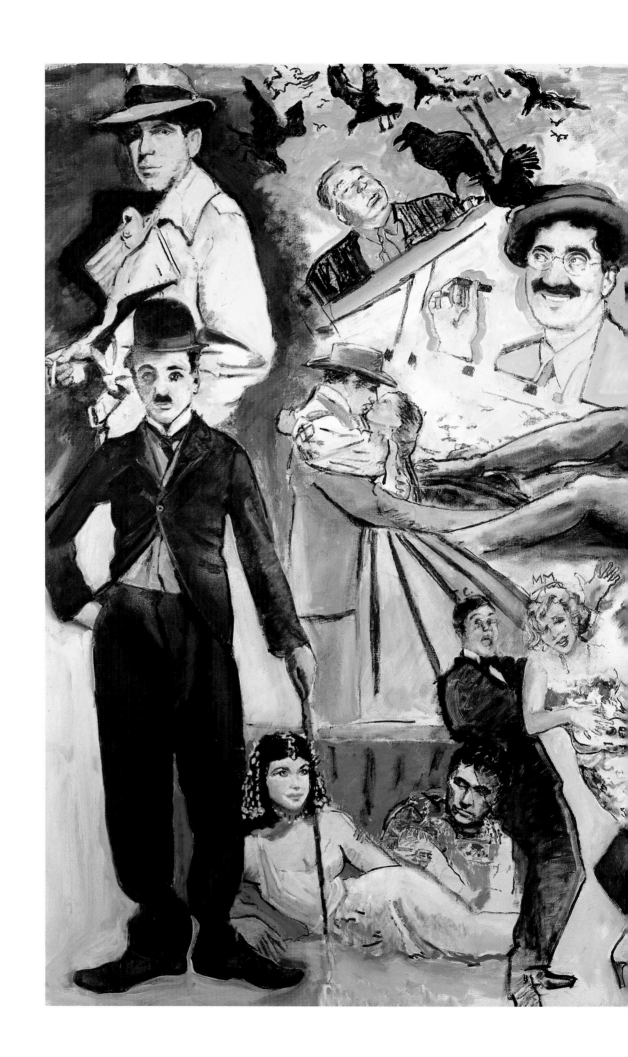

PLATE 58.

History of Hollywood: Part IV

2000, oil on canvas

Larry Rivers '00

List of Plates

PLATE 1

Berdie, 1952
Bronze
67 x 36 x 15 in.
Marlborough Gallery, New York

PLATE 2

Self-Figure, 1953
Oil on canvas
93 3/8 x 65 1/2 in.
The Corcoran Gallery of Art,
Washington, D.C.
Museum Purchase

PLATE 3

Washington Crossing the Delaware,
1953
Oil, graphite, and charcoal on linen
83 5/8 x 111 5/8 in.
Museum of Modern Art, New York
Given Anonymously, 1955

PLATE 4

Berdie Seated, 1953
Bronze sculpture
9 7/8 x 5 x 9 1/4 in.
Collection of the Artist

PLATE 5

Berdie Seated I, 1953
Painted plaster sculpture
10 x 5 x 10 3/8 in.
Collection of the Artist

PLATE 6

O'Hara Nude with Boots, 1954
Oil on canvas
97 x 53 in.
Collection of the Artist

PLATE 7

Portrait of a Man
(John Bernard Myers), 1954
Oil on canvas
25 x 30 3/4 in.
Marlborough Gallery, New York

PLATE 8

The Family, 1954-55
Oil on canvas
82 x 72 in.
Marlborough Gallery, New York

PLATE 9

Boy in Blue Denim
(Portrait of Steven), 1955
Oil on canvas
53 1/2 x 38 in.
The Parrish Art Museum,
Southampton, New York

PLATE 10

Double Portrait of Berdie, 1955
Oil on canvas
70 3/4 x 82 1/2 in.
Whitney Museum of American Art,
New York

PLATE 11

Europe I, 1956
Oil on canvas
72 x 48 in.
The Minneapolis Institute of Arts,
Minnesota
Anonymous Gift

PLATE 12

The 25 Cent Summer Cap, 1956
Oil and charcoal on canvas
53 1/2 x 47 in.
Hirshhorn Museum and Sculpture
Garden, Smithsonian Institution,
Washington, D.C.
Gift of Joseph H. Hirshhorn

PLATE 13

Berdie with the American Flag, 1957
Oil on canvas
20 x 25 7/8 in.
Nelson-Atkins Museum,
Kansas City, Missouri

PLATE 14

Larry Rivers and Frank O'Hara
Stones: Five O'Clock, 1958
Lithograph
19 x 23 1/4 in.
Universal Limited Art Editions

PLATE 15

Larry Rivers and Frank O'Hara
Stones: Berdie, 1959
Lithograph
23 1/4 x 19 in.
Universal Limited Art Editions

PLATE 16

Me in a Rectangle, 1959
Oil on canvas
65 3/4 x 48 3/4 in.
Neuberger Museum, State
University of New York at Purchase
Gift of Jane and Jay Braus

PLATE 17

Three Kings, 1960
Oil on canvas
52 x 60 in.
Collection Andrea Bollt, New York

PLATE 18

The Last Civil War Veteran, 1961
Oil on canvas
82 1/2 x 64 3/4 in.
Anderson Gallery, Buffalo, New York

PLATE 19

French Money, 1961
Oil on canvas
34 x 59 1/2 in.
Private Collection, New York

PLATE 20

Cedar Bar Menu II, 1961
Oil on canvas
48 1/4 x 30 in.
Collection of Mr. and Mrs. Richard
Titelman, Atlanta, Georgia

PLATE 21

Disque Bleu, 1961
Oil on canvas
13 x 13 in.
Collection Richard Shebairo,
New York

PLATE 22

*The Friendship of America and
France (Kennedy and De Gaulle)*
1961-62, repainted 1970
Oil on canvas
51 1/2 x 76 1/2 in.
Collection Marc and Livia Straus

PLATE 23

*Parts of the Face:
French Vocabulary Lesson,* 1961
Oil on canvas
29 1/2 x 29 1/2 in.
Tate Modern Museum, Bankside,
London

PLATE 24

*How to Draw Series: Visage
(Parts of the Face/Two Faces),* 1962
Pencil, collage, and charcoal
on paper
13 3/16 x 16 3/8 in.
Hirshhorn Museum and Sculpture
Garden, Smithsonian Institution,
Washington, D.C.
Gift of Joseph H. Hirshhorn, 1966

PLATE 25

*How to Draw Series:
Oreilles (Ears),* 1962
Gouache, pencil, charcoal, photo-
mechanical reproductions, and
cellophane tape on paper
9 1/4 x 10 3/8 in.
Hirshhorn Museum and Sculpture
Garden, Smithsonian Institution,
Washington, D.C.
Gift of Joseph H. Hirshhorn, 1966

PLATE 26

*How to Draw:
Eyes, Nose, and Mouth,* 1962
Pencil, gouache, collage, and
charcoal on paper
12 15/16 x 14 in.
Hirshhorn Museum and Sculpture
Garden, Smithsonian Institution,
Washington, D.C.
Gift of Joseph H. Hirshhorn, 1966

PLATE 27

Amel Camel, 1962
Oil on canvas on collage
39 x 39 in.
Williams College Museum of Art,
Williamstown, Massachusetts

PLATE 28

French Money, ca. 1962
Drawing
12 1/2 x 14 1/2 in.
Collection Richard Shebairo,
New York

PLATE 29

De Kooning with My Texas Hat, 1963
Pencil, crayon, and cellophane tape
on paper
14 x 16 7/8 in.
Hirshhorn Museum and Sculpture
Garden, Smithsonian Institution,
Washington, D.C.
Gift of Joseph H. Hirshhorn, 1966

PLATE 30

Dutch Masters I
1963
Oil on canvas
40 x 50 in.
Cheekwood Museum of Art,
Nashville, Tennessee

PLATE 31

Dutch Masters and Cigars II, 1963
Oil and board collage on canvas
96 x 67 3/8 in.
The Harry N. Abrams Family
Collection, New York

PLATE 32

The Greatest Homosexual, 1964
Oil, collage, and pencil on canvas
80 x 61 in.
Hirshhorn Museum and Sculpture
Garden, Smithsonian Institution,
Washington, D.C.
Gift of Joseph H. Hirshhorn, 1966

PLATE 48

Dancing with Bomberg's Dancer,
1990
Oil on canvas
70 7/8 x 52 x 2 7/8 in.
Collection David C. Levy,
Washington, D.C.

PLATE 49

Studio Interior, 1990-91
Oil on canvas
60 x 80 in.
Private Collection, New York

PLATE 50

Léger at the Easel: Apache Cap, 1991
Oil on canvas mounted on sculpted
foamcore
63 1/2 x 55 1/2 x 8 1/4 in.
Private Collection, New Jersey

PLATE 51

Art and the Artist:
Picasso and the Bull, 1992
Oil on canvas mounted on sculpted
foamcore
63 x 56 x 6 1/2 in.
Marlborough Gallery, New York

PLATE 52

Art and the Artist: Miró, 1993–95
Oil on canvas mounted on sculpted
foamcore
56 1/2 x 55 x 3 1/4 in.
Marlborough Gallery, New York

PLATE 53

Umber Blues: Sonny and Picasso's
"Three Musicians," 1993
Oil on canvas mounted on sculpted
foamcore
61 x 44 x 5 in.
Collection Risa Meyer, New York

PLATE 54

The Auction, circa 1860, 1993-94
Oil on canvas mounted on sculpted
foamcore
80 x 116 3/4 x 5 in.
The Corcoran Gallery of Art,
Washington, D.C.

PLATE 55

A Vanished World:
Garbo and Gilbert I, 1994
Oil on canvas mounted on sculpted
foamcore
29 1/2 x 42 x 5 in.
Marlborough Gallery, New York

PLATE 56

Déjà Vu and the Red Room:
Double Portrait of Matisse
(Harmony in Red), 1996
Oil on canvas mounted on sculpted
foamcore
63 1/2 x 80 in.
Private Collection, New York

PLATE 57

Tinguely and Rivers in 1978, 1998
Pastel and pencil on paper
22 x 36 in.
Collection of the Artist

PLATE 58

History of Hollywood: Part IV,
2000
Oil on canvas
79 1/2 x 115 in.
Private Collection, New York

Overleaf: **Rivers, 1959** (Walter Silver)

Larry Rivers Chronology

1923. Born Yitzroch Loiza (Irving) Grossberg on August 17 in the Bronx, New York City, the only son and eldest child of Samuel (Shiah) and Shirley (Sonya) Grossberg. His parents were originally from Russia. His father was a plumber and later owned a small trucking company. His father's first love was the fiddle. After selling his trucking business he returned to playing the fiddle at bar mitzvahs and weddings.

1929–40. Attended public schools in the Bronx, including Evander Childs High School, where he watched James Michael Newell paint murals in the school library.

1940. Began musical career as a jazz saxophonist. Changed name to Larry Rivers. The name was given to him by a nightclub emcee who decided to introduce Larry and his band as "Larry Rivers and His Mudcats." His sister insists Rivers borrowed the name from an appellate court judge.

1942. Enlisted in the U.S. Army Air Corps.

1943. Falsely diagnosed with multiple sclerosis and received an honorable medical discharge from the army. Resumed musical career.

1944. Studied composition at the Juilliard School of Music, New York, for one year. Miles Davis, who at the time was living with Charlie Parker, was a fellow student. From 1943 to 1945, Rivers played in jazz bands in and around New York with Shep Fields, Jerry Wald, and Johnny Morris, among others. Met Jack and Jane Freilicher, who introduced Rivers to painting and exposed him to politics, philosophy, and art. Jack impressed him with an image of a bass fiddle by Georges Braque in a book called *The Pocket Book of Modern Art.*

1945. Took first painting lessons during the summer at Old Orchard Beach, Maine, from nineteen-year-old Jane Freilicher, while playing in a band with her husband. Together with Jack, played jazz at various clubs in Brooklyn, the Bronx, and Queens. Married Augusta Burger, the mother of a son, Joseph. Son Steven was born.

Rivers house in the Bronx

Rivers in the army

1946. Went to Miami for the summer with wife, mother-in-law, and sons. Separated from Augusta and moved to an apartment on East Twenty-first Street near the painter Nell Blaine, to whom he was introduced by the Freilichers. Spent two months in a veterans' hospital with hepatitis.

1947. At Blaine's suggestion and with the help of the GI Bill of Rights, Rivers attended Hans Hofmann's school of painting from January 1947 through the summer of 1948 in New York and Provincetown, Massachusetts. Rivers played jazz at the Sea Dragon in Provincetown. Hofmann regularly compared the students' drawings to the work of the old masters. Fellow student was Sam Hunter, who organized a retrospective of Rivers' work in 1965 and wrote two monographs on Rivers.

1948. Began studying education at New York University, intending to support himself by teaching art. William Baziotes was one of his teachers. Became interested in the painting of Pierre Bonnard after seeing the large exhibition of his painting at the Museum of Modern Art. Met Willem de Kooning, Edwin

Denby, Rudolph Burckhardt, and Kenneth Koch.

1949. First one-man exhibition, at the Jane Street Gallery on Madison Avenue in New York. The gallery was an artists' cooperative whose members included Frances Eckstein, Ida Fisher, Al Kresch, Jack Levitan, Luisa Matthiasdottir, and Hyde Solomon. Glowingly reviewed by Clement Greenberg in *The Nation* as an "amazing beginner . . . a better composer of pictures than was Bonnard himself in many instances." Met poet John Ashbery.

1950. Made first trip to France and Italy, spending eight months in Paris. Visited museums with Nell Blaine, and wrote poetry, some of which was published in *Locus Solus* in 1962. Returned to New York and met Franz Kline, Philip Guston, Grace Hartigan, Alfred Leslie, Helen Frankenthaler, and the dealer John Bernard Myers. Met poet Frank O'Hara at party held by John Ashbery. Set up household with mother-in-law, Bertha "Berdie" Burger, who was his favorite model until her death in 1957, and son Steven and stepson Joseph. Berdie's financial assistance allowed him to devote his time almost exclusively to painting. Appeared with John Ashbery and Jane Freilicher in Rudolph Burckhardt's film *Mounting Tension.* Included in *New Talent 1950* show at Kootz Gallery, organized by Meyer Schapiro and Clement Greenberg. Influenced by Chaim Soutine retrospective at the Museum of Modern Art.

1951. Met Jackson Pollock and visited his Long Island studio at The Springs. Began painting first major work, *The Burial,* inspired by Gustave Courbet's *A Burial at Ornans,* 1849-50, and the recent death and funeral of his grandmother. In December, held first of twelve solo exhibitions at John Myers' Tibor de Nagy Gallery in New York. Count Tibor and Myers had established the gallery to exhibit new art by young artists, including Helen Frankenthaler and Robert Goodnough. Granted a bachelor's degree in art education by New York University. Began to spend summers in Southampton, Long Island. Began sculpting in plaster and cement, and made a large figure for Leo Castelli's garden.

1952. Designed sets for the play *Try! Try!,* written by Frank O'Hara, directed by Herbert Machiz, and produced for the Artists' Theater by John Myers. Worked as a caricaturist at the ballpoint pen counter in Bloomingdale's department store, where Rudy Vallee was one of his subjects. Marked the end of his drawing in pen. Had one-man show and was included in a group exhibition at Tibor de Nagy Gallery.

1953. Completed *Washington Crossing the Delaware,* a controversial painting based on the 1851 painting by Emanuel Leutze in the Metropolitan Museum of Art. In 1955, the painting was acquired by the Museum of Modern Art, his first to be acquired by a major museum. Also completed *Self-Figure.* Moved

from New York to Southampton, Long Island, and began to use Fairfield Porter's barn as a studio. In his autobiography Rivers described his escape this way: "I wanted to get away from it all. To do my paintings more seriously without any of the interruptions of the city." Read "21 novels of Balzac, Stendhal and all the Russians." Appeared in Rudolph Burckhardt's film *A Day in the Life of a Cleaning Woman.* Exhibited in one-man exhibition at Tibor de Nagy Gallery.

1954. Gloria Vanderbilt Foundation acquired *The Burial,* on the advice of art historian Meyer Schapiro, for the Fort Wayne Art School and Museum, Fort Wayne, Indiana. First exhibition of sculpture at the Stable Gallery, New York. With O'Hara, wrote a play *Kenneth Koch: A Tragedy* mimicking Koch's writing style to parody him and other regulars at the Cedar Bar.

1955. Awarded third prize in the *Twenty-fourth Corcoran Biennial Exhibition of Contemporary American Oil Paintings,* Washington, D.C., for *Self-Figure,* which was acquired by the Corcoran Gallery of Art. *Double Portrait of Berdie* was exhibited in *U.S. Painting: Some Recent Directions* at the Stable Gallery.

1956. One of twelve artists who represented the United States at the *IV Bienal do Museo de Arte Moderna de São Paulo,* São Paulo, Brazil. Adopted stepson Joseph. Bought house in Southampton. Included in *12 Americans* and *Recent Drawings U.S.A.,* shows organized by the Museum of Modern Art. Metropolitan Museum of Art acquired *The Sitter,* and Joseph Hirshhorn acquired several works from Rivers' one-man show at Tibor de Nagy Gallery.

1957. Began making welded metal sculpture. Collaborated with Frank O'Hara on twelve lithographs combining illustration and poetry. O'Hara wrote his poetry on the lithograph stones surrounded by Rivers' images. This portfolio, *Stones,* was completed and printed in 1959, the first major project for Tatyana Grosman, founder of Universal Limited Art Editions (ULAE) print studio. Berdie Burger died on Labor Day at age 66. Won $32,000 on the TV quiz show *The $64,000 Question.* Returned with sons to live in Second Avenue apartment. Had one-man exhibition at Tibor de Nagy Gallery. Directed Kenneth Koch's poetry and jazz series at the Five Spot.

1958. Spent a month in Paris, playing in several jazz bands. *Washington Crossing the Delaware* was damaged in a fire at the Museum of Modern Art. Exhibited in one-man show at Tibor de Nagy Gallery.

1959. Having frequented the Cedar Bar Tavern, a local artists' hangout,

for many years, wrote a poem that he wrapped in one of the tavern's menus. Painted *Cedar Bar Menu I.* Appeared with Allen Ginsberg and Jack Kerouac in film *Pull My Daisy,* by Robert Frank and Alfred Leslie. Exhibited painting-poems with Grace Hartigan at Tibor de Nagy Gallery. Initiated series of paintings relating to photographs of Civil War veterans.

1960. Began collaboration with poet Kenneth Koch on painting-poems, *New York 1950–60, Post Cards,* and *Shoes.* Painted *Cedar Bar Menu II.* Wrote review of Monet show at Museum of Modern Art for *ARTNews.* Acted in Jack Gelber's *The Connection* at the Living Theater, about New York's downtown drug culture, and in Kenneth Koch's *The Election,* in which Rivers played Lyndon Johnson. Exhibited at Tibor de Nagy Gallery. Painted second painting

Rivers and Clarice on their wedding day, 1961

entitled *Washington Crossing the Delaware,* which was acquired by the Whitney Museum of American Art. Started series of paintings based on playing cards and cigarette packages.

1961. Married Clarice Price, a Welsh-born teacher of music and art, in London. Painted in Paris from October to July 1962, where he began *French Money, Webster Cigar Box,* and *Vocabulary Lessons* series. The *Vocabulary Lessons* series parodied more traditional nude paintings by adding labels identifying various body parts. Met, collaborated with, and became friends with Jean Tinguely and Niki de Saint-Phalle. Charcoal and pencil drawing of a Buick was reproduced for the cover of March issue of *Art International.* Exhibited sculpture at Martha Jackson Gallery, New York, and painting at the Dwan Gallery,

Los Angeles, and Tibor de Nagy Gallery.

1962. The first Rivers-Tinguely collaboration, *The Friendship of America and France,* was shown at the Musée des Arts Décoratifs, Paris. London's Tate Gallery purchased *Parts of the Face: French Vocabulary Lesson.* With the help of artist Yves Klein, had show at Galerie Rive Droite, Paris, which John Ashbery reviewed for *Art International.* Exhibited at Gimpel Fils Gallery in London and spoke on contemporary painting at Royal Albert Hall.

1963. Joined Marlborough-Gerson Gallery, New York. John Myers, director of his former gallery, Tibor de Nagy, served him with a summons for breach of contract. Completed commission on minority group theme, *The Identification Manual.* Began *Dutch Masters* series. Also

Rivers at work in his studio, 1965
(Camilla McGrath)

completed a billboard commissioned for the First New York Film Festival at Lincoln Center. The maquette was purchased by Joseph Hirshhorn.

1964. Journeyed to London, where he was an artist-in-residence at the Slade School of Fine Arts, University of London, from January through June. Also traveled through France, Spain, and Morocco. Exhibited at Gimpel Fils Gallery, London. Returned to New York and South-ampton in June. Designed sets for two one-act plays, *The Toilet* and *The Slave,* by LeRoi Jones, performed at the St. Mark's Playhouse, New York. Daughter Gwynne born. Completed *The Greatest Homosexual,* Rivers' own version of a famous portrait,

Rivers with children (from left)
Gwynne, Joseph, and Steven
in Southampton, 1966
(Camilla McGrath)

The Emperor Napoleon in His Study (1812) by Jacques-Louis David. Later he would do a second version of this painting, entitled *The Second Greatest Homosexual.*

1965–66. First comprehensive retrospective exhibition of 170 works, organized by Sam Hunter and shown at Rose Art Museum, Brandeis University, Waltham, Massachusetts. Exhibition traveled to Pasadena Art Museum, Detroit Institute of Arts, Minneapolis Institute of Arts, and the Jewish Museum, New York. Worked on *The History of the Russian Revolution from Marx to Mayakovsky,* which was first exhibited in the Jewish Museum, as part of the retro-spective

1966. Designed sets and costumes for Stravinsky's *Oedipus Rex,* performed by the New York Philharmonic at Lincoln Center, under the direction of Lukas Foss.

Death of friend and collaborator Frank O'Hara. Daughter Emma born. Spent winter of 1966–67 in Belgravia section of London. Made cover illustration for John Gruen's *The New Bohemia.*

1967. Separated from Clarice Price. Traveled to Africa to make television documentary film *Africa and I* with Pierre Dominique Gaisseau. Traveled through Kenya, Nigeria, the Congo, Ethiopia, Rwanda, Tanzania, and other countries. Participated in the Museum of Modern Art's memorial exhibition *In Memory of My Feelings* for the late poet and curator Frank O'Hara.

1968. Rivers' father died. Made second trip to Africa with Gaisseau to complete documentary film. Narrowly escaped death in Lagos, Nigeria, when an army officer ordered them executed as suspected white mercenaries in Nigerian civil war. Imprisoned and later released

after execution order was withdrawn. Returned to New York. Completed monumental murals *The Boston Massacre* and *The Paul Revere Event* for New England Merchants National Bank of Boston.

1969. Completed multimedia construction *Forty Feet of Fashion,* a commission for the Smith Haven Mall in Lake Grove, Long Island. Began working with spray paint.

1970. Completed *Some American History* for the Menil Foundation, Houston. The series featured subjects relating to African American history, including portraits of famous African Americans Frederick Douglas, W.E.B. Du Bois, Malcolm X, and LeRoi Jones (Amiri Baraka). Lived and worked in New York City and Southampton. Moved to airbrush painting and the use of acrylics. Began working with video. Marlborough Gallery held its first Rivers solo exhibition. Showed drawings in *Larry Rivers: Drawings 1949–1969* at Art Institute of Chicago and Smith College. Made illustrations for Kenneth Koch's *When the Sun Tries to Go On.*

1971. Traveled through Oregon and California. Rice University, Houston, exhibited Rivers' works from *Some American History.* Exhibited drawings, collages, and prints at Heath Gallery, Atlanta.

1972. Returned to California with Diana Molinari and taped video segments for an operatic treatment of Kenneth Koch's poem "The Artist," which was performed at the Whitney Museum of American Art, New York. Taught at the University of California at Santa Barbara.

1973. Traveled to Sweden for group show at the Swedish Museum of Modern Art, Stockholm, where his work *Living at the Movies* was exhibited. Began series of paintings entitled *The Coloring Book of Japan.* Made studies for illustrations used in Kenneth Koch's *Art of Love.* Exhibited in one-man exhibitions at Marlborough Gallery and Palais des Beaux-Arts, Brussels.

1974. Completed the Japanese series, shown at Marlborough Gallery, New York. Began to teach art at the Parsons School of Design.

1975. Traveled to Africa, where he made a short video with Peter Beard. Commissioned to paint the *Beauty and the Beast* series.

1976. Traveled to Russia at the invitation of the Union of Soviet Artists, where he lectured in several cities on contemporary American art. Made videotapes during the trip.

1977. Began using color carbon. Started a series of works based on Rembrandt's *Polish Rider,* from which the Hirshhorn Museum and Sculpture Garden, Washington, D.C., acquired *Rainbow Rembrandt.* Completed *The Donkey and the Darling,* a book of fifty-two lithographs, in collaboration with writer Terry Southern. Had one-man exhibitions at Marlborough and

Robert Miller galleries in New York and Gimpel Fils Gallery in London.

1978. Commissioned by Jeffrey Loria to paint the *Golden Oldies* series, which included vignettes of his own works of the 1950s and 1960s. Part of the series was shown at ACA Galleries, New York.

1979. Completed the *Golden Oldies* series. Said Rivers: "I'm concentrating on, as Edmund Wilson said, 'touching the superlative' in my own work." Traveled to Paris; Jean Tinguely commissioned *May, 1968* series. Collaborated with Carol Brightman on publication of *Drawings and Digressions,* a book of Rivers' drawings accompanied by his commentary.

1980. Retrospective exhibition held at Museo de Arte Contemporáneo, Caracas, Venezuela.

1980–81. Traveling retrospective exhibition at Kestner-Gesellschaft, Hannover; Kunstverein, Munich; Kunsthalle, Tübingen; and Staatliche Kunsthalle, Berlin. Visited Caracas for USICA (U.S. International Communication Agency).

1981. Began living with artist Daria Deshuk.

1982. *The Continuing Interest in Abstract Art* series shown at F.I.A.C. (Grand Palais, Paris), Marlborough Fine Art, London, and Marlborough Gallery, New York. Jeffrey and Sivia Loria, collectors of Rivers' art, commissioned *History of Matzoh: The Story of the Jews.* This painting, later expanded, depicts the history of the Jews from Moses to Theodore Herzl. Rivers was criticized for not making it a serious painting; he responded by saying, "In Jewish history there's a humorous way of looking at things. There are many responses to it, but there is a way of looking at it like this. I think there is a sad, tragic part of it, but that's not the only way to look at it." Appeared in Marshall Brickman's film *Lovesick.* Exhibited at Studio Marconi, Milan.

1983. Completed eleven-color lithograph *Garbo Grosman* in tribute to Tatyana Grosman. Thirty-year survey exhibition held at Guild Hall Museum, East Hampton, New York, and Lowe Art Museum, Coral Gables, Florida. Also exhibited at Elaine Horwich Gallery, Phoenix.

1984. The mural *Philadelphia Now and Then* completed for J.C. Penney, Philadelphia. Exhibited at Kouros Gallery, New York.

1984–85. *History of Matzoh: The Story of the Jews* exhibited in one-man exhibition at the Jewish Museum, New York.

1985. Son Sam Deshuk Rivers born.

1986. Completed a computer art project for the BBC, London, also shown in the United States. Solo exhibition of new relief paintings at Marlborough Gallery. Continued interest in the portrayal of dancers with the painting of modern dancer Merce Cunningham. Produced a commissioned cover for the *New York Times Magazine, Erasing the Past*, using concentration camp imagery. Interest in the Holocaust and the writings of Primo Levi resulted in a set of three large portraits of Levi. Exhibited at Marlborough Fine Art, Tokyo; Adelphi University Center, Garden City, New York; Jan Turner Gallery, Los Angeles; Heland-Thorden-Wetterling Gallery, Stockholm; and Marlborough Gallery, New York.

1987. Traveled to the Dominican Republic to work on *Umber Blues.* Reviewed Ronald Sukenick's book *Down & In* for the *New York Times.* Commissioned by the Philadelphia Historical Society to make a print celebrating the Bicentennial of the U.S. Constitution. Contributed a special eight-page project to *Artforum's* November issue, "1000 Avant-Garde Plays," by Kenneth Koch. Created a cover design for the *Art at the Armory* catalog based on Duchamp's *Nude Descending a Staircase.*

1988. Began a series of large versions of Duchamp's *Nude Descending a Staircase,* entitled *75 Years Later.* Included in Spoleto

Festival U.S.A. exhibition held at the Gibbs Art Gallery, Charleston, South Carolina. Italian television broadcast an interview with Rivers regarding his paintings of the Italian writer Primo Levi for its program *What's Happening in America.*

1989. Began a series of reliefs depicting Webster cigar boxes, seated figures, and Charlie Chaplin. Placed Chaplin and other subjects against the backgrounds of paintings by Fernand Léger.

1990. Created new reliefs based on images of Fred Astaire and Courbet's *The Artist's Studio,* in which Rivers showed himself surrounded by images of his own paintings. Rivers became interested in photographs of Auschwitz and painted his Holocaust theme painting *Four Seasons: Fall in the Forest of Birkenau* (later renamed *Spring in the Forest of Birkenau* by Rivers). Retrospective *Larry Rivers:*

Public and Private, organized by the Butler Institute of American Art and the American Federation of Arts, toured six U.S. cities from 1990 to 1992. Solo exhibition entitled *Works from the Sixties* shown at Marlborough Gallery.

1991. Continued *Art and the Artist* series based on works by Matisse and other modern artists, including Léger, Mondrian, and Picasso. A retrospective of prints and multiples toured ten U.S. cities from 1991 to 1992.

1992. Created works based on depictions of family friends and objects in the studio. Nassau County Museum of Art, Long Island, organized retrospective of paintings, drawings, prints, and sculpture shown from August through November 1992. First one-man exhibition in Rome held at Gabbiano Gallery. Exhibition *Larry Rivers: Master Prints 1957–1992* held at Galerie Hertz, Louisville, Kentucky. Published his autobiography, *What Did I Do?,* coauthored with Arnold Weinstein. Began studying Yiddish.

1993. Exhibited *A Vanished Life* series, including works featuring Greta Garbo and her leading men.

1994. At Marlborough Gallery, exhibited a series of works called *The Auction and Other Visions of Slavery* in which a monumental painting, *The Auction, circa 1860,* depicts a slave auction through the eyes of a nineteenth-century artist. The accompanying drawings

depict other images of African American life.

1998. Painted *Fashion and the Birds* series, combining imagery from fashion magazines and the bird studies of John James Audubon, playing on the idea of the vanity of plumage and apparel. A retrospective of Rivers' 1970s and 1980s work, *Larry Rivers: The Artist in the Labyrinth,* was exhibited at Philharmonic Galleries in Naples, Florida.

1999. Began work on the series *History of Hollywood.* Exhibition held at Marlborough Gallery entitled *Fashion;* a number of the works were pastel or flat paintings. Commissioned to illustrate *New York Times* article on composer Sir Edward Elgar.

2001. *Fashion Show Monte Carlo 2001* series displayed in the windows of Lord and Taylor, New York, continued his theme of fashion. Continued to play the saxophone in jazz bands.

2002. Performed at daughter Gwynne's wedding. Retrospective exhibition at Corcoran Gallery of Art.

One-Man Exhibitions

1949. Jane Street Gallery, New York

1951. Tibor de Nagy Gallery, New York

1952. Tibor de Nagy Gallery, New York

1953. Tibor de Nagy Gallery, New York

1954. Stable Gallery, New York (sculpture); Tibor de Nagy Gallery, New York

1955–60. Tibor de Nagy Gallery, New York

1961. Martha Jackson Gallery, New York (sculpture); Tibor de Nagy Gallery, New York; Dwan Gallery, Los Angeles

1962. Tibor de Nagy Gallery, New York; Gimpels Fils, London; Galerie Rive Droite, Paris

1963. Dwan Gallery, Los Angeles

1964. Gimpels Fils, London

1965–66. Traveling retrospective exhibition: Rose Art Museum, Brandeis University, Waltham, Massachusetts; Pasadena Art Museum, Pasadena, California; The Jewish Museum, New York; The Detroit Institute of Arts; The Minneapolis Institute of Arts

1970. The Art Institute of Chicago (drawings)

1970–71. Marlborough Gallery, New York

1973. Marlborough Gallery, New York

1973–74. Palais des Beaux-Arts, Brussels, Belgium

1974–75. Marlborough Gallery, New York

1976. Gimpel Fils, London

1977. Marlborough Gallery, New York; Robert Miller Gallery, New York; Gimpel Fils, London

1978. ACA Galleries, New York

1979. Marlborough Gallery, New York

1980–82. Traveling retrospective exhibition: Kestner-Gesellschaft, Hannover; Kunstverein, Munich; Kunsthalle, Tübingen; Staatliche Kunsthalle, Berlin, Germany

1981–82. Traveling exhibition: F.I.C.A., Paris; Marlborough Fine Art (London) Ltd.; Marlborough Gallery, New York

1982. Marlborough Gallery, New York; Studio Marconi, Milan, Italy

1983. Elaine Horwich Gallery, Phoenix, Arizona; Guild Hall Museum, East Hampton, New York; Lowe Art Museum, Coral Gables, Florida

1984. Kouros Gallery, New York

1984–85. The Jewish Museum, New York

1985. Museum of the University of Pennsylvania, Philadelphia

1985–86. Marlborough Fine Art, Tokyo

1986. Adelphi University Center, Garden City, New York; Jan Turner Gallery, Los Angeles; Marlborough Gallery, New York

1987. Simms Fine Art, New Orleans

1988. Spoleto Festival U.S.A., Gibbs Art Gallery, Charleston, South Carolina

1988–89. Marlborough Gallery, New York

1990. Marlborough Fine Art, London; Marlborough Gallery, New York; Galerie Beaubourg, Paris; Fandos Galería de Arte Moderno, Valencia, Spain

1990–92. Traveling exhibition: The Butler Institute of American Art, Youngstown, Ohio; Norton Gallery of Art, West Palm Beach, Florida; Fort Wayne Museum of Art, Fort Wayne, Indiana; Scottsdale Center for the Arts, Scottsdale, Arizona; J. B. Speed Art Museum, Louisville, Kentucky

1991. Galeria Antonio Machon, Madrid

1991–92. Traveling print exhibition: Elaine Horwich Gallery, Scottsdale, Arizona, and Santa Fe, New Mexico; Gallery 454 North, Los Angeles; The Remba Gallery, Santa Monica, California; Magidson Gallery, Aspen, Colorado; Marilyn Wilson Gallery, Birmingham, Alabama; The Hokin Gallery, Miami; Robert Stein Fine Art, St. Louis; Hokin/Kaufman Gallery, Chicago; Nassau County Museum of Art, Roslyn Harbor, New York

1992. Nassau County Museum of Art, Roslyn Harbor, New York; Galleria d'Arte Il Gabbiano, Rome, Italy

1993. Marlborough Gallery, New York; Galería Marlborough, Madrid

1994. Marlborough Gallery, New York

1997. Marlborough Gallery, New York

1999. *Fashion Show,* Marlborough Gallery, New York

2001. *Fashion Show Monte Carlo 2001,* Lord and Taylor, New York and Marlborough Monte Carlo

2002. Retrospective: Corcoran Gallery of Art, Washington, D.C.

Rivers' Southampton studio

Public Collections

"Not one day of my life have I wasted in searching for the truth." "I remember everything I know, even the most superficial things. And what comes out is in my canvases." "I was energetic and egomaniacal and, what is more important, cocky and angry enough ..." "It's history that makes a person something."

Designed by Susan Marsh

Typeset by Matt Mayerchak

in ITC Bodoni and Meta

Printed by Dr. Cantz'sche Druckerei